Charles Heath

The Waverley Gallery of the Principal Female Characters

in Sir Walter Scott's Romances

.

Charles Heath

The Waverley Gallery of the Principal Female Characters
in Sir Walter Scott's Romances

ISBN/EAN: 9783337038328

Printed in Europe, USA, Canada, Australia, Japan

Cover: Foto ©Thomas Meinert / pixelio.de

More available books at **www.hansebooks.com**

THE

WAVERLEY GALLERY

OF THE

Principal Female Characters

IN

SIR WALTER SCOTT'S ROMANCES.

FROM ORIGINAL PAINTINGS BY EMINENT ARTISTS—ENGRAVED UNDER
THE SUPERINTENDENCE OF CHARLES HEATH.

NEW YORK:
D. APPLETON AND COMPANY,
443 & 445 BROADWAY.
1866.

THE WOMEN OF WAVERLEY.

The Women of the Waverley Novels form a family of
beauties interesting to us for almost every reason that can
render women interesting. The "story of their lives from
year to year" has been read the wide world over, and
there are but few readers of the English language who cannot remember, looking not far back in thought, perhaps, an
even especial tenderness for one or more of them. They are
beings with whom we have hoped and feared with a reality
so intense, that they have become part of the experience of
our lives. Taken simply as the studies of a great literary
master, they appeal to all our gentler feelings with a warmth
unequalled by any other imaginary sisterhood; they are
second in any thing only to the heroines of Shakspeare, and
to them only in the exquisite ideality with which those
dainty beings are pictured.

To please our natural love of pictures with a glimpse at
the possible faces of these women—to show the ideas that
artists skilled in all the niceties of plastic expression form

from the great master's descriptions—is the object of this gallery. This has always been regarded as one of the sun-shiny walks of art. Except in the case of that sublime countenance of Homer, which, though originally only the imagination of a Greek artist, has now become the accepted type of the poet, we know of no instance in which the se-verer labor of the pencil has been turned in this direction ; but, on the contrary, it has been rather the painter's recrea-tion. And as such a lighter labor of art, associated from its very beginning with happy thoughts, and the pleasanter mo-ments of life, this Gallery is deemed a most appropriate Holiday Offering.

CONTENTS.

		PAGE
FLORA MAC-IVOR,	WAVERLEY,	9
MISS BRADWARDINE,	WAVERLEY,	19
JULIA MANNERING,	GUY MANNERING,	25
MISS WARDOUR,	ANTIQUARY,	29
DIANA VERNON,	ROB ROY,	45
HELEN MAC-GREGOR,	ROB ROY,	51
ISABELLA VERE,	BLACK DWARF,	59
JENNY DENNISON,	OLD MORTALITY,	67
EDITH BELLENDEN,	OLD MORTALITY,	75
JEANIE DEANS,	HEART OF MID LOTHIAN,	81
EFFIE DEANS,	HEART OF MID LOTHIAN,	87
MADGE WILDFIRE,	HEART OF MID LOTHIAN,	93
LUCY ASHTON,	BRIDE OF LAMMERMOOR,	99
LADY ROWENA,	IVANHOE,	105
REBECCA,	IVANHOE,	111
THE WHITE LADY OF AVENEL,	MONASTERY,	117
CATHERINE SEYTON,	ABBOT,	129
JANET FOSTER,	KENILWORTH,	137
AMY ROBSART,	KENILWORTH,	139
MINNA TROIL,	PIRATE,	143

8 CONTENTS.

PAGE

MARGARET RAMSAY, . . . FORTUNES OF NIGEL, 147

ALICE BRIDGENORTH, . . PEVERIL OF THE PEAK, 155

JACQUELINE, ... QUENTIN DURWARD, . 159

CLARA MOWBRAY, . . ST. RONAN'S WELL, . 163

THE UNKNOWN, ... REDGAUNTLET, . . 165

GREENMANTLE, . . REDGAUNTLET, . 167

RACHAEL GEDDES, . . REDGAUNTLET, . 171

ROSE FLAMMOCK, . . . BETROTHED, . . 173

EVELINE BERENGER, . . BETROTHED, . . . 177

QUEEN BERENGARIA, . . TALISMAN, . 183

ALICE LEE, ... WOODSTOCK, . . . 189

GLEE MAIDEN, ... FAIR MAID OF PERTH, 197

CATHERINE, ... FAIR MAID OF PERTH, 211

ANNE OF GEIERSTEIN, . . ANNE OF GEIERSTEIN, . 217

LADY AUGUSTA BERKELY, . CASTLE DANGEROUS, . 223

ZILIA DE MONÇADA, . . SURGEON'S DAUGHTER, . 227

THE

WAVERLEY GALLERY.

FLORA MAC-IVOR.

WHEN Waverley had been a guest at Tully-Veolan nearly
six weeks, he descried, one morning, as he took his usual walk
before the breakfast-hour, signs of uncommon perturbation in
the family. Four bare-legged dairy-maids, with each an empty
milk-pail in her hand, ran about with frantic gestures, and
uttering loud exclamations of surprise, grief, and resentment.
From their appearance, a pagan might have conceived them a
detachment of the celebrated Belides, just come from their bale-
ing penance. As nothing was to be got from this distracted
chorus, excepting "Lord guide us!" and "Eh, sirs!" ejacula-
tions which threw no light upon the cause of their dismay,
Waverley repaired to the fore-court, as it was called, where he
beheld Bailie Macwheeble cantering his white pony down the
avenue with all the speed it could muster. He had arrived, it
would seem, upon a hasty summons, and was followed by half a
score of peasants from the village, who had no great difficulty
in keeping pace with him.

2

Waverley took his way to the breakfast parlor, where he found Rose, who seemed vexed and thoughtful. A single word explained the mystery. "Your breakfast will be a disturbed one, Captain Waverley. A party of Caterans have come down upon us last night, and have driven off all our milch cows."

"A party of Caterans?"

"Yes; robbers from the neighboring Highlands. We used to be quite free from them while we paid black-mail to Fergus Mac-Ivor Vich Ian Vohr; but my father thought it unworthy of his rank and birth to pay it any longer, and so this disaster has happened."

And such were the circumstances under which the young captain first heard the name of Mac-Ivor. Coupling it as they did with robbery and violence, they were not calculated to prepossess the mind in favor of any one bearing it; yet he became interested in hearing of the strange life and character of the Highland Chief—conversed with the Baron of Highland robbers generally—and listened with something of wonder to Rose when she said of the chieftain's sister: "Flora is one of the most beautiful and accomplished young ladies in this country: she was bred in a convent in France, and was a great friend of mine before this unhappy dispute." An opportunity to go into the Highlands presented itself, and Waverley went. The most notable result of the excursion was his meeting with the lady of whom Rose spoke so warmly, to whom he was presented by her brother upon retiring from a formal banquet at the chief's table.

The drawing-room of Flora Mac-Ivor was furnished in the plainest and most simple manner; for at Glennaquoich every other sort of expenditure was retrenched as much as possible, for the purpose of maintaining, in its full dignity, the hospitality of the chieftain, and retaining and multiplying the number of his dependants and adherents. But there was no appearance of this parsimony in the dress of the lady herself, which was in texture elegant, and even rich, and arranged in a manner which partook partly of the Parisian fashion, and partly of the more simple dress of the Highlands, blended together with great taste. Her hair was not disfigured by the art of the friseur, but fell in jetty ringlets on her neck, confined only by a circlet, richly set with diamonds. This peculiarity she adopted in compliance with the Highland prejudices, which could not endure that a woman's head should be covered before wedlock.

Flora Mac-Ivor bore a most striking resemblance to her brother Fergus; so much so, that they might have played Viola and Sebastian with the same exquisite effect produced by the appearance of Mrs. Henry Siddons and her brother, Mr. William Murray, in these characters. They had the same antique and regular correctness of profile; the same dark eyes, eyelashes, and eye-brows; the same clearness of complexion, excepting that Fergus's was embrowned by exercise, and Flora's possessed the utmost feminine delicacy. But the haughty, and somewhat stern regularity of Fergus's features, was beautifully softened in those of Flora. Their voices were also similar in tone, though differing in the key. That of Fergus, especially while issuing orders to his followers during their military exercise, reminded Edward of a favorite passage in the description of Emetrius:

——— whose voice was heard around,
Loud as a trumpet with a silver sound.

That of Flora, on the contrary, was soft and sweet, "an excellent thing in woman;" yet, in urging any favorite topic, which she often pursued with natural eloquence, it possessed as well the tones which impress awe and conviction, as those of persuasive insinuation. The eager glance of the keen black eye, which, in the chieftain, seemed impatient even of the material obstacles it encountered, had, in his sister, acquired a gentle pensiveness. His looks seemed to seek glory, power, all that could exalt him above others in the race of humanity ; while those of his sister, as if she were already conscious of mental superiority, seemed to pity, rather than envy, those who were struggling for any farther distinction. Her sentiments corresponded with the expression of her countenance. Early education had impressed upon her mind, as well as on that of the chieftain, the most devoted attachment to the exiled family of Stuart. She believed it the duty of her brother, of his clan, of every man in Britain, at whatever personal hazard, to contribute to that restoration which the partisans of the Chevalier St. George had not ceased to hope for. For this she was prepared to do all, to suffer all, to sacrifice all. But her loyalty, as it exceeded her brother's in fanaticism, excelled it also in purity. Accustomed to petty intrigue, and necessarily involved in a thousand paltry and selfish discussions, ambitious also by nature, his political faith was tinctured, at least, if not tainted, by the views of interest and advancement so easily combined with it; and at the moment he should unsheathe his claymore, it might be difficult to say whether it would be most with the view of making James Stuart a king, or Fergus Mac-Ivor an earl. This, indeed, was a mixture of feeling which he did not avow even to himself, but it existed, nevertheless, in a powerful degree.

In Flora's bosom, on the contrary, the zeal of loyalty burnt pure and unmixed with any selfish feeling ; she would have as soon made religion the mask of ambitious and interested views, as have shrouded them under the opinions which she had been taught to think patriotism. Such instances of devotion were not uncommon among the followers of the unhappy race of Stuart, of which many memorable proofs will recur to the mind of most of my readers. But peculiar attention on the part of the Chevalier de St. George and his princess to the parents of Fergus and his sister, and to themselves, when orphans, had riveted their faith. Fergus, upon the death of his parents, had been for some time a page of honor in the train of the chevalier's lady, and, from his beauty and sprightly temper, was uniformly treated by her with the utmost distinction. This was also extended to Flora, who was maintained for some time at a convent of the first order, at the princess's expense, and removed from thence into her own family, where she spent nearly two years. Both brother and sister retained the deepest and most grateful sense of her kindness.

Having thus touched upon the leading principle of Flora's character, I may dismiss the rest more slightly. She was highly accomplished, and had acquired those elegant manners to be expected from one who, in early youth, had been the companion of a princess ; yet she had not learned to substitute the gloss of politeness for the reality of feeling. When settled in the lonely regions of Glennaquoich, she found that her resources in French, English, and Italian literature, were likely to be few and interrupted ; and, in order to fill up the vacant time, she bestowed a part of it upon the music and poetical traditions of the Highlanders, and began really to feel the pleasure in the pursuit, which her brother, whose perceptions of literary merit were more blunt, rather affected for the sake of popularity than actually experienced. Her resolution was strengthened in these

researches, by the extreme delight which her inquiries seemed
to afford those to whom she resorted for information.

Her love of her clan, an attachment which was almost
hereditary in her bosom, was, like her loyalty, a more pure passion than that of her brother.   He was too thorough a politician,
regarded his patriarchal influence too much as the means of ac-
complishing his own aggrandizement, that we should term him
the model of a Highland Chieftain.   Flora felt the same anxiety
for cherishing and extending their patriarchal sway, but it was
with the generous desire of vindicating from poverty, or at least
from want and foreign oppression, those whom her brother was
by birth, according to the notions of the time and country, entitled
to govern.

To this young lady, presiding at the female empire of the
tea-table, Fergus introduced Captain Waverley, whom she received with the usual forms of politeness.

Flora, like every beautiful woman, was conscious of her own
power, and pleased with its effects, which she could easily discern, from the respectful, yet confused address of the young soldier.   But, as she possessed excellent sense, she gave the romance
of the circumstances under which he appeared, and other acci-
dental circumstances, full weight in appreciating the feelings
with which Waverley seemed obviously to be impressed ; and
unacquainted with the fanciful and susceptible peculiarities of
his character, considered his homage as the passing tribute which
a woman of even inferior charms might have expected in such
a situation.

But that night, as may readily be conceived by the reader,
who knows him better, Edward retired with his mind agitated
by a variety of new and conflicting feelings, which detained
him from rest for some time, in that not unpleasing state of

mind in which fancy takes the helm, and the soul rather drifts passively along with the rapid and confused tide of reflection, than exerts itself to encounter, systematize, or examine them. At a late hour he fell asleep, and dreamed of Flora Mac-Ivor.

It was not in a life like Flora's that love could come, as Waverley very soon learned. Filled with the pride of her race and the glory of the cause in which her brother was embarked, she had nothing to yield to gentler feeling; and receiving with quiet courtesy the young soldier's suit, she freely said—" I could esteem you, Mr. Waverley, as much, perhaps more, than any man I have ever seen ; but I cannot love you as you ought to be loved."

After the young soldier's departure from Glennaquoich, he scarcely saw Flora until the day preceding that upon which her brother was to be executed for high treason—when, having reached Carlisle, where the trial had taken place, he immediately sent word of his intention to wait upon her that evening. The messenger brought back a letter, in Flora's beautiful Italian hand, which seemed scarce to tremble, even under its load of misery. " Miss Flora Mac-Ivor," the letter bore, " could not refuse to see the dearest friend of her dear brother, even in her present circumstances of unparalleled distress."

When Edward reached Miss Mac-Ivor's present place of abode, he was instantly admitted. In a large and gloomy tapestried apartment, Flora was seated by a latticed window, sewing what seemed to be a garment of white flannel. At a little distance sat an elderly woman, apparently a foreigner, and of a religious order. She was reading in a book of Catholic devotion, but when Waverley entered, laid it on the table, and left the room. Flora rose to receive him, and stretched out her hand, but neither ventured to attempt speech. Her fine complexion

was totally gone; her person considerably emaciated; and her
face and hands as white as the purest statuary marble, forming
a strong contrast with her sable dress and jet-black hair. Yet,
amid these marks of distress, there was nothing neglected or
ill-arranged about her attire; even her hair, though totally without ornament, was disposed with her usual attention to neatness.
The first words she uttered were, "Have you seen him?"

"Alas, no," answered Waverley, "I have been refused ad-
mittance."

"It accords with the rest," she said; "but we must submit.
Shall you obtain leave, do you suppose?"

"For—for—to-morrow," said Waverley; but muttering the
last word so faintly that it was almost unintelligible.

"Ay, then or never," said Flora, "until"—she added, looking upward, "the time when, I trust, we shall all meet. But I
hope you will see him while earth yet bears him. He always loved
you at his heart, though—but it is vain to talk of the past."

"Vain, indeed!" echoed Waverley.

"Or, even of the future, my good friend," said Flora, "so
far as earthly events are concerned; for how often have I pictured to myself the strong possibility of this horrid issue, and
tasked myself to consider how I could support my part; and yet
how far has all my anticipations fallen short of the unimaginable
bitterness of this hour!"

"Dear Flora, if your strength of mind"——

"Ay, there it is," she answered, somewhat wildly; "there
is, Mr. Waverley, there is a busy devil at my heart, that whispers—but it were madness to listen to it—that the strength of
mind on which Flora prided herself has murdered her brother!"

"Good God! how can you give utterance to a thought so
shocking?"

"Ay, is it not so? but yet it haunts me like a phantom; I know it is unsubstantial and vain; but it *will* be present; will intrude its horrors on my mind; will whisper that my brother, as volatile as ardent, would have divided his energies amid a hundred objects. It was I who taught him to concentrate them, and to gage all on this dreadful and desperate cast. Oh, that I could recollect that I had but once said to him, ' He that striketh with the sword shall die by the sword;' that I had but once said, Remain at home; reserve yourself, your vassals, your life, for enterprises within the reach of man. But oh, Mr. Waverley, I spurred his fiery temper, and half of his ruin at least lies with his sister!"

The horrid idea which she had intimated, Edward endeavored to combat by every incoherent argument that occurred to him. He recalled to her the principles on which both thought it their duty to act, and in which they had been educated.

"Do not think I have forgotten them," she said, looking up, with eager quickness; "I do not regret his attempt, because it was wrong! oh no! on that point I am armed; but because it was impossible it could end otherwise than thus."

"Yet it did not always seem so desperate and hazardous as it was; and it would have been chosen by the bold spirit of Fergus, whether you had approved it or no; your counsels only served to give unity and consistence to his conduct; to dignify, but not to precipitate, his resolution." Flora had soon ceased to listen to Edward, and was again intent upon her needle-work.

"Do you remember," she said, looking up with a ghastly smile, "you once found me making Fergus's bride-favors, and now I am sewing his bridal-garment. Our friends here," she continued, with suppressed emotion, " are to give hallowed earth in their chapel to the bloody relics of the last Vich Ian Vohr. But they

3

will not all rest together; no—his head!—I shall not have the
last miserable consolation of kissing the cold lips of my dear,
dear Fergus!"

The unfortunate Flora here, after one or two hysterical sobs,
fainted in her chair. The lady, who had been attending in the
anteroom, now entered hastily, and begged Edward to leave the
room, but not the house.

When he was recalled, after the space of nearly half an hour,
he found that, by a strong effort, Miss Mac-Ivor had greatly
composed herself. It was then he ventured to urge Miss Bradwardine's claim, to be considered as an adopted sister, and em-
powered to assist her plans for the future.

"I have had a letter from my dear Rose," she replied, "to
the same purpose. Sorrow is selfish and engrossing, or I would
have written to express, that even in my own despair, I felt a
gleam of pleasure at learning her happy prospects, and at hearing that the good old baron has escaped the general wreck.
Give this to my dearest Rose; it is her poor Flora's only ornament of value, and was the gift of a princess." She put into
his hands a case, containing the chain of diamonds with which she
used to decorate her hair. "To me it is in future useless. The
kindness of my friends has secured me a retreat in the convent
of the Scottish Benedictine nuns in Paris. To-morrow—if indeed I can survive to-morrow—I set forward on my journey
with this venerable sister. And now, Mr. Waverley, adieu!
May you be as happy with Rose as your amiable dispositions
deserve : and think sometimes on the friends you have lost. Do
not attempt to see me again ; it would be mistaken kindness."

ROSE BRADWARDINE.

MISS BRADWARDINE was but seventeen ; yet, at the last races of the county town of ———, upon her health being proposed among a round of beauties, the Laird of Bumper-quaigh, permanent toast-master and croupier of the Bauther-whillery Club, not only said *More* to the pledge in a pint bumper of Bourdeaux, but, ere pouring forth the libation, de-nominated the divinity to whom it was dedicated, " the Rose of Tully-Veolan ; " upon which festive occasion, three cheers were given by all the sitting members of that respectable society, whose throats the wine had left capable of such exertion. Nay, I am well assured, that the sleeping partners of the company snorted applause, and that although strong bumpers and weak brains had consigned two or three to the floor, yet even these, fallen as they were from their high estate, uttered divers inar-ticulate sounds, intimating their assent to the motion.

Such unanimous applause could not be extorted but by ac-knowledged merit ; and Rose Bradwardine not only deserved it, but also the approbation of much more rational persons than the Bautherwhillery Club could have mustered, even before dis-cussion of the first *magnum.* She was indeed a very pretty girl,

Jf the Scotch cast of beauty, that is, with a profusion of hair
of paley gold, and a skin like the snow of her own mountains
in whiteness. Yet she had not a pallid or pensive cast of countenance ; her features, as well as her temper, had a lively expression ; her complexion, though not florid, was so pure as to
seem transparent, and the slightest emotion sent her whole blood
at once to her face and neck. Her form, though under the com·
mon size, was remarkably elegant, and her motions light, easy,
and unembarrassed. Her father had taught her French and
Italian, and a few of the ordinary authors in those languages
ornamented her shelves. He had endeavored also to be her
preceptor in music ; but as he began with the more abstruse
doctrines of the science, and was not perhaps master of them
himself, she had made no proficiency farther than to be able to
accompany her voice with the harpsichord ; but even this was not
very common in Scotland at that period. To make amends,
she sung with great taste and feeling, and with a respect to the
sense of what she uttered, that might be proposed in example
to ladies of much superior musical talent. Her natural good
sense taught her, that if, as we are assured by high authority,
music be " married to immortal verse," they are very often di-
vorced by the performer in a most shameful manner. It was
perhaps owing to this sensibility to poetry, and power of com-
bining its expression with those of the musical notes, that her
singing gave more pleasure to all the unlearned in music, and
even to many of the learned, than could have been communicated by a much finer voice and more brilliant execution, un-
guided by the same delicacy of feeling.

A bartizan, or projecting gallery, before the windows of her
parlor, served to illustrate another of Rose's pursuits ; for it was
crowded with flowers of different kinds, which she had taken

under her special protection. A projecting turret gave access to this Gothic balcony, which commanded a most beautiful prospect. The view of an old tower, or fortalice, introduced some family anecdotes and tales of Scottish chivalry, which the Baron told with great enthusiasm. The projecting peak of an impending crag which rose near it, had acquired the name of St. Swithin's Chair, and Rose was called upon to sing a little legend, in which some superstitions relating to it had been interwoven by a village poet.

I conjecture the following copy of this legend to have been somewhat corrected by Waverley, to suit the taste of those who might not relish pure antiquity :

ST. SWITHIN'S CHAIR.

On Hallow-Mass Eve, ere ye boune ye to rest,
Ever beware that your couch be bless'd ;
Sign it with cross, and sain it with bead,
Sing the Ave, and say the Creed.

For on Hallow-Mass Eve the Night-Hag will ride,
And all her nine-fold sweeping on by her side,
Whether the wind sing lowly or loud,
Sailing through moonshine or swath'd in the cloud.

The Lady she sat in St. Swithin's Chair,
The dew of the night had damp'd her hair:
Her cheek was pale—but resolved and high
Was the word of her lip and the glance of her eye.

She mutter'd the spell of Swithin bold,
When his naked foot traced the midnight wold,
When he stopp'd the Hag as she rode the night
And bade her descend, and her promise plight.

He that dare sit on St. Swithin's Chair,
When the Night-Hag wings the troubled air,
Questions three, when he speaks the spell,
He may ask, and she must tell.

The Baron has been with King Robert his liege,
These three long years in battle and siege;
News are there none of his weal or his wo,
And fain the lady his fate would know.

She shudders and stops as the charm she speaks :—
Is it the moody owl that shrieks ?
Or is it that sound, betwixt laughter and scream,
The voice of the Demon who haunts the stream ?

The moan of the wind sunk silent and low,
And the roaring torrent has ceased to flow ;
The calm was more dreadful than raging storm,
When the cold gray mist brought the ghastly Form !
*   *   *   *   *   *

"I am sorry to disappoint the company, especially Captain
Waverley, who listens with such laudable gravity; it is but a
fragment, although I think there are other verses, describing the
return of the baron from the wars, and how the lady was found
'clay-cold upon the grounsill ledge.'"

"It is one of those figments," observed Mr. Bradwardine,
"with which the early history of distinguished families was de-
formed in the times of superstition: as that of Rome, and other
ancient nations, had their prodigies, sir, the which you may read
in ancient histories, or in the little work compiled by Julius
Obsequens, and inscribed by the learned Scheffer, the editor, to
his patron, Benedictus Skytte, Baron of Dudershoff."

"My father has a strange defiance of the marvellous, Captain Waverley," observed Rose, "and once stood firm when a whole synod of Presbyterian divines were put to the rout by a sudden apparition of the foul fiend."

Waverley looked as if desirous to hear more.

"Must I tell my story as well as sing my song? Well— Once upon a time there lived an old woman, called Janet Gellatley, who was suspected to be a witch, on the infallible grounds that she was very old, very ugly, very poor, and had two sons, one of whom was a poet and the other a fool, which visitation, all the neighborhood agreed, had come upon her for the sin of witchcraft. And she was imprisoned for a week in the steeple of the parish church, and sparely supplied with food, and not permitted to sleep, until she herself became as much persuaded of her being a witch as her accusers ; and in this lucid and happy state of mind was brought forth to make a clean breast, that is, to make open confession of her sorceries, before all the Whig gentry and ministers in the vicinity, who were no conjurors themselves. My father went to see fair play between the witch and the clergy ; for the witch had been born on his estate. And while the witch was confessing that the Enemy appeared, and made his addresses to her as a handsome black man—which, if you could have seen poor old blear-eyed Janet, reflected little honor on Apollyon's taste—and while the auditors listened with astonished ears, and the clerk recorded with a trembling hand, she, all of a sudden, changed the low mumbling tone with which she spoke into a shrill yell, and exclaimed, ' Look to yourselves ! look to yourselves ! I see the Evil One sitting in the midst of ye.' The surprise was general, and terror and flight its immediate consequences. Happy were those who were next the door ; and many were the disasters that befell hats, bands, cuffs, and wigs, before they could get out of the church, where

they left the obstinate prelatist to settle matters with the witch
and her admirer, at his own peril or pleasure."

This anecdote led into a long discussion of

> All those idle thoughts and fantasies,
> Devices, dreams, opinions, unsound,
> Shows, visions, soothsays, and prophecies,
> And all that feigned is, as leasings, tales and lies.

Yet Rose Bradwardine, beautiful, amiable, and cultivated as
we have described her, had not precisely the sort of beauty or
merit, which captivates a romantic imagination in early youth.
She was too frank, too confiding, too kind ; amiable qualities, un-
doubtedly, but destructive of the marvellous, with which a youth
of imagination delights to dress the empress of his affections.

"That man," Flora Mac-Ivor had said, "will find an inestimable treasure in the affections of Rose Bradwardine, who shall
be so fortunate as to become their object.   Her very soul is in
home, and in the discharge of all those quiet virtues of which
home is the centre.   Her husband will be to her what her father
now is, the object of all her care, solicitude, and affection.   She
will see nothing, and connect herself with nothing, but by him
and through him.   If he is a man of sense and virtue, she will
sympathize in his sorrows, divert his fatigue, and share his pleasures.   If she becomes the property of a churlish or negligent husband, she will suit his taste also, for she will not long survive his
unkindness.   And, alas ! how great is the chance, that some such
unworthy lot may be that of my poor friend !   O that I were a
queen this moment and could command the most amiable and
worthy youth of my kingdom to accept happiness with the hand
of Rose Bradwardine."

JULIA MANNERING.

At length the trampling of horses, and the sound of wheels, were heard. The servants, who had already arrived, drew up in the hall to receive their master and mistress, with an importance and *empressement*, which, to Lucy, who had never been accustomed to society, or witnessed what is called the manners of the great, had something alarming. Mac-Morlan went to the door to receive the master and mistress of the family, and in a few moments they were in the drawing-room.

Mannering, who had travelled as usual on horseback, entered with his daughter hanging upon his arm. She was of the middle size, or rather less, but formed with much elegance : piercing dark eyes, and jet-black hair of great length, corresponded with the vivacity and intelligence of features, in which were blended a little haughtiness, and a little bashfulness, a great deal of shrewdness, and some power of humorous sarcasm. " I shall not like her," was the result of Lucy Bertram's first glance; " and yet I rather think I shall," was the thought excited by the second.

Miss Mannering was furred and mantled up to the throat against the severity of the weather ; the Colonel in his military greatcoat. He bowed to Mrs. Mac-Morlan, whom his daughter

4

also acknowledged with a fashionable courtesy, not dropped so low as at all to incommode her person. The Colonel then led his daughter up to Miss Bertram, and, taking the hand of the latter, with an air of great kindness, and almost paternal affection, he said, "Julia, this is the young lady whom I hope our good friends have prevailed on to honor our house with a long visit. I shall be much gratified indeed if you can render Woodbourne as pleasant to Miss Bertram, as Ellangowan was to me when I first came as a wanderer into this country."

The young lady courtesied acquiescence, and took her new friend's hand. Mannering now turned his eye upon the Dominie, who had made bows since his entrance into the room, sprawling out his leg, and bending his back like an automaton, which continues to repeat the same movement until the motion is stopped by the artist. "My good friend, Mr. Sampson," said Mannering, introducing him to his daughter, and darting at the same time a reproving glance at the damsel, notwithstanding he had himself some disposition to join her too obvious inclination to risibility. "This gentleman, Julia, is to put my books in order when they arrive, and I expect to derive great advantage from his extensive learning."

"I am sure we are obliged to the gentleman, papa, and, to borrow a ministerial mode of giving thanks, I shall never forget the extraordinary countenance he has been pleased to show us. But, Miss Bertram," continued she, hastily, for her father's brows began to darken, "we have travelled a good way,—will you permit me to retire before dinner?"

This intimation dispersed all the company, save the Dominie, who, having no idea of dressing but when he was to rise, or of undressing but when he meant to go to bed, remained by himself, chewing the cud of a mathematical demonstration, until the company again assembled in the drawing-room, and from thence adjourned to the dining-parlor.

When the day was concluded, Mannering took an opportunity to hold a minute's conversation with his daughter in private.

"How do you like your guests, Julia?"

"Oh, Miss Bertram of all things—but this is a most original parson—why, dear sir, no human being will be able to look at him without laughing."

"While he is under my roof, Julia, every one must learn to do so."

"Lord, papa, the very footmen could not keep their gravity!"

"Then let them strip off my livery," said the Colonel, "and laugh at their leisure. Mr. Sampson is a man whom I esteem for his simplicity and benevolence of character."

"Oh, I am convinced of his generosity too," said this lively lady; "he cannot lift a spoonful of soup to his mouth without bestowing a share on every thing round."

"Julia, you are incorrigible; but remember, I expect your mirth on this subject to be under such restraint, that it shall neither offend this worthy man's feelings, nor those of Miss Bertram, who may be more apt to feel upon his account than he on his own. And so, good night, my dear; and recollect, that though Mr. Sampson has certainly not sacrificed to the graces, there are many things in this world more truly deserving of ridicule than either awkwardness of manners or simplicity of character."

MISS WARDOUR.

SIR ARTHUR and his daughter had set out, according to their
first proposal, to return to Knockwinnock by the turnpike road;
but, when they reached the head of the loaning, as it was called,
or great lane, which on one side made a sort of avenue to the
house of Monkbarns, they discerned, a little way before them,
Lovel, who seemed to linger on the way as if to give him an opportunity to join them. Miss Wardour immediately proposed
to her father that they should take another direction; and, as
the weather was fine, walk home by the sands, which, stretching
below a picturesque ridge of rocks, afforded at almost all times
a pleasanter passage between Knockwinnock and Monkbarns
than the high-road.

Sir Arthur acquiesced willingly, and they soon attained the
side of the ocean. The tide was by no means so far out as they
had computed; but this gave them no alarm; there were seldom
ten days in the year when it approached so near the cliffs as not
to leave a dry passage. But, nevertheless, at periods of spring-
tide, or even when the ordinary flood was accelerated by high
winds, this road was altogether covered by the sea; and tradi-
tion had recorded several fatal accidents which had happened on

such occasions. Still, such dangers were considered as remote and improbable ; and rather served, with other legends, to amuse the hamlet fireside, than to prevent any one from going between Knockwinnock and Monkbarns by the sands.

As Sir Arthur and Miss Wardour paced along, enjoying the pleasant footing afforded by the cool, moist, hard sand, Miss Wardour could not help observing, that the last tide had risen considerably above the usual water-mark. Sir Arthur made the same observation, but without its occurring to either of them to be alarmed at the circumstance. The sun was now resting his huge disk upon the edge of the level ocean, and gilded the accumulation of towering clouds through which he had travelled the livelong day, and which now assembled on all sides, like misfortunes and disasters around a sinking empire and falling monarch. Still, however, his dying splendor gave a sombre magnificence to the massive congregation of vapors, forming out of their unsubstantial gloom the show of pyramids and towers, some touched with gold, some with purple, some with a hue of deep and dark red. The distant sea, stretched beneath this varied and gorgeous canopy, lay almost portentously still, reflecting back the dazzling and level beams of the descending luminary, and the splendid coloring of the clouds amidst which he was setting. Nearer to the beach, the tide rippled onward in waves of sparkling silver, that imperceptibly, yet rapidly, gained upon the sand.

Many wild birds, with the instinct which sends them to seek the land before a storm arises, were now winging towards their nests with the shrill and dissonant clang which announces disquietude and fear. The disk of the sun became almost totally obscured ere he had altogether sunk below the horizon, and an early and lurid shade of darkness blotted the serene twilight of a summer evening. The wind began next to arise; but its wild and moaning sound was heard for some time, and its effects became visible on the bosom of the sea, before the gale was felt on shore. The mass of waters, now dark and threatening, began to lift itself in larger ridges, and sink in deeper furrows, forming waves that rose high in foam upon the breakers, or burst upon the beach with a sound resembling distant thunder.

Appalled by this sudden change of weather, Miss Wardour drew close to her father, and held his arm fast. " I wish," at length she said, but almost in a whisper, as if ashamed to express her increasing apprehensions—" I wish we had kept the road we intended, or waited at Monkbarns for the carriage."

Sir Arthur looked round, but did not see, or would not acknowledge, any signs of an immediate storm. They would reach Knockwinnock, he said, long before the tempest began. But the speed with which he walked, and with which Isabella could hardly keep pace, indicated a feeling that some exertion was necessary to accomplish his consolatory prediction.

They were now near the centre of a deep but narrow bay, or recess, formed by two projecting capes of high and inaccessible rock, which shot out into the sea like the horns of a crescent; and neither durst communicate the apprehension which each began to entertain, that, from the unusually rapid advance of the tide, they might be deprived of the power of proceeding by doubling the promontory which lay before them, or of retreating by the road which brought them thither.

As they thus pressed forward, longing doubtless to exchange the easy curving line, which the sinuosities of the bay compelled them to adopt, for a straighter and more expeditious path, though less conformable to the line of beauty, Sir Arthur observed a

human figure on the beach advancing to meet them. "Thank
God," he exclaimed, "we shall get round Halket-head! that
person must have passed it; " thus giving vent to the feeling
of hope, though he had suppressed that of apprehension.

"Thank God, indeed!" echoed his daughter, half audibly,
half internally, as expressing the gratitude which she strongly
felt.

The figure which advanced to meet them made many signs,
which the haze of the atmosphere, now disturbed by wind and
by a drizzling rain, prevented them from seeing or comprehending
distinctly. Some time before they met, Sir Arthur could recog-
nize the old blue-gowned beggar, Edie Ochiltree. It is said
that even the brute creation lay aside their animosities and an-
tipathies when pressed by an instant and common danger. The
beach under Halket-head, rapidly diminishing in extent by the
encroachments of a spring-tide and a north-west wind, was in
like manner a neutral field, where even a justice of peace and
a strolling mendicant might meet upon terms of mutual for-
bearance.

"Turn back! turn back!" exclaimed the vagrant; "why
did ye not turn when I waved to you?"

"We thought," replied Sir Arthur, in great agitation—"we
thought we could get round Halket-head."

"Halket-head! The tide will be running on Halket-head,
by this time, like the Fall of Fyers! It was a' I could do to get
round it twenty minutes since—it was coming in three feet
abreast. We will maybe get back by Bally-burgh Ness Point
yet. The Lord help us, it's our only chance. We can but try."

"My God, my child!"—"My father, my dear father!"
exclaimed the parent and daughter, as, fear lending them strength
and speed, they turned to retrace their steps, and endeavored to

double the point, the projection of which formed the southern extremity of the bay.

"I heard ye were here, frae the bit callent ye sent to meet your carriage," said the beggar, as he trudged stoutly on a step or two behind Miss Wardour, "and I couldna bide to think of the dainty young leddy's peril, that has aye been kind to ilka forlorn heart that cam near her. Sae I lookit at the lift and the rin o' the tide, till I settled it that if I could get down time enough to gie you warning, we wad do weel yet. But I doubt, I doubt I have been beguiled! for what mortal ee ever saw sic a race as the tide is rinning e'en now? See, yonder's the Ratton's Skerry—he aye held his neb abune the water in my day—but he's aneath it now."

Sir Arthur cast a look in the direction in which the old man pointed. A huge rock, which in general, even in spring-tides, displayed a hulk, like the keel of a large vessel, was now quite under water, and its place only indicated by the boiling and breaking of the eddying waves which encountered its submarine resistance.

The waves had now encroached so much upon the beach, that the firm and smooth footing which they had hitherto had on the sand must be exchanged for a rougher path close to the foot of the precipice, and in some places even raised upon its lower ledges. It would have been utterly impossible for Sir Arthur Wardour, or his daughter, to have found their way along these shelves without the guidance and encouragement of the beggar, who had been there before in high tides, though never, he acknowledged, "in sae awsome a night as this."

Each minute did their enemy gain ground perceptibly upon them! Still, however, loath to relinquish the last hopes of life, they bent their eyes on the black rock pointed out by Ochiltree.

5

It was yet distinctly visible among the breakers, and continued to be so, until they came to a turn in their precarious path, where an intervening projection of rock hid it from their sight. Deprived of the view of the beacon on which they had relied, they now experienced the double agony of terror and suspense. They struggled forward, however; but, when they arrived at the point from which they ought to have seen the crag, it was no longer visible. The signal of safety was lost among a thousand white breakers, which, dashing upon the point of the promontory, rose in prodigious sheets of snowy foam, as high as the mast of a first-rate man-of-war, against the dark brow of the precipice.

The countenance of the old man fell. Isabella gave a faint shriek, and, "God have mercy upon us!" which her guide solemnly uttered, was piteously echoed by Sir Arthur—"My child! my child!—to die such a death!"

"My father! my dear father!" his daughter exclaimed, clinging to him,—"and you, too, who have lost your own life in endeavoring to save ours!"

"That's not worth the counting," said the old man. "I hae lived to be weary o' life; and here or yonder—at the back o' a dike, in a wreath o' snaw, or in the wame o' a wave, what signifies how the auld gaberlunzie dies?"

"Good man," said Sir Arthur, "can you think of nothing?—of no help?—I'll make you rich—I'll give you a farm—I'll "——

"Our riches will be soon equal," said the beggar, looking out upon the strife of the waters—"they are sae already; for I hae nae land, and you would give your fair bounds and barony for a square yard of rock that would be dry for twal hours."

While they exchanged these words, they paused upon the highest ledge of rock to which they could attain; for it seemed that any further attempt to move forward could only serve to anticipate their fate. Here, then, they were to await the sure though slow progress of the raging element, something in the situation of the martyrs of the early church, who, exposed by heathen tyrants to be slain by wild beasts, were compelled for a time to witness the impatience and rage by which the animals were agitated, while awaiting the signal for undoing their grates, and letting them loose upon the victims.

Yet even this fearful pause gave Isabella time to collect the powers of a mind naturally strong and courageous, and which rallied itself at this terrible juncture. "Must we yield life," she said, "without a struggle? Is there no path, however dreadful, by which we could climb the crag, or at least attain some height above the tide, where we could remain till morning, or till help comes? They must be aware of our situation, and will raise the country to relieve us."

Sir Arthur, who heard, but scarcely comprehended, his daughter's question, turned, nevertheless, instinctively and eagerly to the old man, as if their lives were in his gift. Ochiltree paused. " I was a bauld craigsman," he said, " ance in my life, and mony a kittywake's and lungie's nest hae I harried up amang thae very black rocks ; but it's lang, lang syne, and nae mortal could speel them without a rope—and if I had ane, my ee-sight, and my footstep, and my handgrip, hae a' failed mony a day sinsyne—and then how could I save *you ?*—but there was a path here ance, though maybe, if we could see it, ye would rather bide where we are. His name be praised ! " he ejaculated suddenly, " there's ane coming down the crag e'en now ! " Then, exalting his voice, he hilloa'd out to the daring adventurer such instructions as his former practice, and the remembrance of local circumstances, suddenly forced upon his

mind : " Ye're right—ye're right !—that gate, that gate !—fas-
ten the rope weel round Crummie's-horn, that's the muckle black
stane—cast twa plies round it—that's it !—now weize yoursell a
wee easel-ward—a wee mair yet to that ither stane—we ca'd it
the Cat's-lug—there used to be the root o' an aik-tree there
—that will do!—canny now, lad—canny now—tak tent and
tak time—Lord bless ye, tak time.—Vera weel !—Now ye maun
get to Bessy's Apron, that's the muckle braid flat blue stane
—and then, I think, wi' your help and the tow thegither, I'll
win at ye, and then we'll be able to get up the young leddy and
Sir Arthur."

The adventurer, following the directions of old Edie, flung
down the end of the rope, which the old man secured around
Miss Wardour, wrapping her previously in his own blue gown,
to preserve her as much as possible from injury. Then, avail-
ing himself of the rope, which was made fast at the other end,
he began to ascend the face of the crag—a most precarious and
dizzy undertaking, which, however, after one or two perilous
escapes, placed him safe on the broad flat stone beside our friend
Lovel. Their joint strength was able to raise Isabella to the
place of safety which they had attained. Lovel then descended
in order to assist Sir Arthur, around whom he adjusted the rope;
and again mounting to their place of refuge, with the assistance
of old Ochiltree, and such aid as Sir Arthur himself could afford,
he raised him beyond the reach of the billows.

"The lassie—the puir sweet lassie," said the old man;
" mony such a night have I weathered at hame and abroad, but,
God guide us, how can she ever win through it ! "

His apprehension was communicated in smothered accents
to Lovel; for, with the sort of free-masonry by which bold and
ready spirits correspond in moments of danger, and become

almost instinctively known to each other, they had established a
mutual confidence.—"I'll climb up the cliff again," said Lovel,
"there's day-light enough left to see my footing; I'll climb up,
and call for more assistance.

"Do so, do so, for heaven's sake!" said Sir Arthur, eagerly.

"Are ye mad?" said the mendicant; "Francie o' Fowls-
heugh, and he was the best craigsman that ever speel'd heugh,
(mair by token, he brake his neck upon the Dunbuy of Slaines,)
wadna hae ventured upon the Halket-head craigs after sundown.
—It's God's grace, and a great wonder besides, that ye are not
in the middle o' that roaring sea wi' what ye hae done already.
—I didna think there was the man left alive would hae come
down the craigs as ye did. I question an I could hae done it
mysell, at this hour and in this weather, in the youngest and
yaldest of my strength.—But to venture up again—it's a mere
and a clear tempting o' Providence."

"I have no fear," answered Lovel; "I marked all the stations
perfectly as I came down, and there is still light enough left to
see them quite well—I am sure I can do it with perfect safety.
Stay here, my good friend, by Sir Arthur and the young lady."

"Deil be in my feet then," answered the bedesman sturdily;
"if ye gang, I'll gang too; for between the twa o' us, we'll hae
mair than wark eneugh to get to the tap o' the heugh."

"No, no—stay you here and attend to Miss Wardour—you
see Sir Arthur is quite exhausted."

"Stay yoursell then, and I'll gae," said the old man; "let
death spare the green corn and take the ripe."

"Stay both of you, I charge you," said Isabella, faintly, "I
am well, and can spend the night very well here—I feel quite
refreshed." So saying, her voice failed her—she sunk down,
and would have fallen from the crag, had she not been supported

by Lovel and Ochiltree, who placed her in a posture half sitting, half reclining, beside her father, who, exhausted by fatigue of body and mind so extreme and unusual, had already sat down on a stone in a sort of stupor.

"It is impossible to leave them," said Lovel. "What is to be done?—Hark! hark!—Did I not hear a halloo?"

"The skriegh of a Tammie Norie," answered Ochiltree, "I ken the skirl weel."

"No, by Heaven," replied Lovel, "it was a human voice."

A distant hail was repeated, the sound plainly distinguish-able among the various elemental noises, and the clang of the sea mews by which they were surrounded. The mendicant and Lovel exerted their voices in a loud halloo, the former waving Miss Wardour's handkerchief on the end of his staff to make them conspicuous from above. Though the shouts were repeat-ed, it was some time before they were in exact response to their own, leaving the unfortunate sufferers uncertain whether, in the darkening twilight and increasing storm, they had made the persons who apparently were traversing the verge of the preci-pice to bring them assistance, sensible of the place in which they had found refuge. At length their halloo was regularly and distinctly answered, and their courage confirmed, by the assur-ance that they were within hearing, if not within reach, of friendly assistance.

The shout of human voices from above was soon augmented, and the gleam of torches mingled with those lights of evening which still remained amidst the darkness of the storm. Some attempt was made to hold communication between the assistants above, and the sufferers beneath, who were still clinging to their precarious place of safety; but the howling of the tempest limited their intercourse to cries, as inarticulate as those of the winged denizens of the crag, which shrieked in chorus, alarmed by the reiterated sound of human voices, where they had seldom been heard.

"I see them," said Oldbuck, "I see them low down on that flat stone—Hilli-hilloa, hilli-ho-a!"

"I see them mysell weel eneugh," said Mucklebackit; "they are sitting down yonder like hoodlecraws in a mist; but d'ye think ye'll help them wi' skirling that gate like an auld skart before a flaw o' weather? Steenie, lad, bring up the mast.—Odd, I'se hae them up as we used to boust up the kegs o' gin and brandy lang syne.—Get up the pick-axe, make a step for the mast—make the chair fast with the rattlin—haul taut and belay!"

The fishers had brought with them the mast of a boat, and as half of the country fellows about had now appeared either out of zeal or curiosity, it was soon sunk in the ground and sufficiently secured. A yard, across the upright mast, and a rope stretched along it, and reeved through a block at each end, formed an extempore crane, which afforded the means of lowering an arm-chair well secured and fastened down to the flat shelf on which the sufferers had roosted. Their joy at hearing the preparations going on for their deliverance was considerably qualified when they beheld the precarious vehicle, by means of which they were to be conveyed to upper air. It swung about a yard free of the spot which they occupied, obeying each impulse of the tempest, the empty air all around it, and depending upon the security of a rope, which, in the increasing darkness, had dwindled to an almost imperceptible thread. Besides the hazard of committing a human being to the vacant atmosphere in such a slight means of conveyance, there was the fearful danger of the chair and its occupant being dashed, either by the wind or the vibrations of the cord, against the rugged face of the precipice. But to diminish the risk as much as possible, the experienced seamen had let down with the chair another line, which, being attached to it, and held by the persons beneath, might serve by way of *gy*, as Mucklebackit expressed it, to render its descent in some measure steady and regular. Still, to commit one's self in such a vehicle, through a howling tempest of wind and rain, with a beetling precipice above, and a raging abyss below, required that courage which despair alone can inspire. Yet wild as the sounds and sights of danger were, both above, beneath, and around, and doubtful and dangerous as the mode of escaping appeared to be, Lovel and the old mendicant agreed, after a moment's consultation, and after the former, by a sudden strong pull, had, at his own imminent risk, ascertained the security of the rope, that it would be best to secure Miss Wardour in the chair, and trust to the tenderness and care of those above for her being safely craned up to the top of the crag.

"Let my father go first!" exclaimed Isabella; "for God's sake, my friends, place him first in safety!"

"It cannot be, Miss Wardour," said Lovel; "your life must be first secured—the rope which bears your weight may—"

"I will not listen to a reason so selfish!"

"But ye maun listen to it, my bonny lassie," said Ochiltree; "for a' our lives depend on it; besides, when ye get on the tap o' the heugh yonder, ye can gie them a round guess o' what's ganging on in this Patmos o' ours—and Sir Arthur's far by that, as I am thinking."

Struck with the truth of this reasoning, she exclaimed, "True, most true; I am ready and willing to undertake the first risk. What shall I say to our friends above?"

"Just to look that their tackle does not graze on the face o'
tne craig, and to let the chair down, and draw it up hooly
and fairly—we will halloo when we are ready."

With the sedulous attention of a parent to a child, Lovel
bound Miss Wardour with his handkerchief, neckcloth, and the
mendicant's leathern belt, to the back and arms of the chair,
ascertaining accurately the security of each knot, while Ochiltree
kept Sir Arthur quiet. "What are ye doing wi' my bairn?—
What are ye doing?—She shall not be separated from me—
Isabel, stay with me, I command you."

"Lordsake, Sir Arthur, haud your tongue, and be thankful
to God that there's wiser folk than you to manage this job!"
cried the beggar, worn out by the unreasonable exclamations of
the poor baronet.

"Farewell, my father," murmured Isabella—"farewell, my
—my friends;" and, shutting her eyes, as Edie's experience recommended, she gave the signal to Lovel, and he to those who
were above. She rose, while the chair in which she sat was
kept steady by the line which Lovel managed beneath. With a
beating heart he watched the flutter of her white dress, until the
vehicle was on a level with the brink of the precipice.

"Canny now, lads, canny now!" exclaimed old Mucklebackit, who acted as commodore; "swerve the yard a bit.—Now
—there! there she sits safe on dry land!"

A loud shout announced the successful experiment to her
fellow-sufferers beneath, who replied with a ready and cheerful
halloo. Monkbarns, in his ecstasy of joy, stripped his greatcoat to wrap up the young lady, and would have pulled off his
coat and waistcoat for the same purpose, had he not been withheld by the cautious Caxon. "Haud a care o' us, your honor
will be killed wi' the hoast—ye'll no get out o' your night-cowl

6

this fortnight—and that will suit us unco ill.—Na, na—there's the chariot down by, let two o' the folk carry the young leddy there."

"You're right," said the Antiquary, readjusting the sleeves and collar of his coat, "you're right, Caxon; this is a naughty night to swim in.—Miss Wardour, let me convey you to the chariot."

"Not for worlds till I see my father safe."

In a few distinct words, evincing how much her resolution had surmounted even the mortal fear of so agitating a hazard, she explained the nature of the situation beneath, and the wishes of Lovel and Ochiltree.

"Right, right, that's right too—I should like to see the son of Sir Gamelyn de Guardover on dry land myself—I have a notion he would sign the abjuration oath, and the Ragman-rool to boot, and acknowledge Queen Mary to be nothing better than she should be, to get alongside my bottle of old port that he ran away from, and left scarce begun. But he's safe now, and here a' comes—(for the chair was again lowered, and Sir Arthur made fast in it, without much consciousness on his own part,) here a' comes—bowse away, my boys—canny wi' him—a pedigree of a hundred links is hanging on a tenpenny tow—the whole barony of Knockwinnock depends on three plies of hemp —*respice finem, respice funem*—look to your end—look to a rope's end.—Welcome, welcome, my good old friend, to firm land, though I cannot say to warm land or to dry land—a cord forever against fifty fathom of water, though not in the sense of the base proverb—a fico for the phrase—better *sus. per funem*, than *sus. per coll.*"

While Oldbuck ran on in this way, Sir Arthur was safely wrapped in the close embraces of his daughter, who, assuming that

authority which the circumstances demanded, ordered some of
the assistants to convey him to the chariot, promising to follow
in a few minutes. She lingered on the cliff, holding an old
countryman's arm, to witness probably the safety of those whose
dangers she had shared.

"What have we here?" said Oldbuck, as the vehicle once
more ascended. "What patched and weather-beaten matter is
this?" Then, as the torches illumined the rough face and gray
hairs of old Ochiltree,—"What! is it thou?—come, old Mocker,
I must needs be friends with thee—but who the devil makes up
your party besides?"

"Ane that's weel worth ony twa o' us Monkbarns—it's the
young stranger lad they ca' Lovel—and he's behaved this blessed
night as if he had three lives to rely on, and was willing to waste
them a' rather than endanger ither folk's.—Ca' hooly, sirs, as ye
wad win an auld man's blessing!—mind there's naebody below
now to haud the gy.—Hae a care o' the Cat's-lug corner—bide
weel aff Crummie's-horn!"

"Have a care indeed," echoed Oldbuck; "what! is it my
rara avis—my black swan—my phœnix of companions in a
post-chaise?—take care of him Mucklebackit."

"As muckle care as if he were a graybeard o' brandy; and
I canna take mair if his hair were like John Harlowe's.—Yo, ho,
my hearts, bowse away with him!"

Lovel did, in fact, run a much greater risk than any of his
precursors. His weight was not sufficient to render his ascent
steady amid such a storm of wind, and he swung like an agitated
pendulum at the mortal risk of being dashed against the rocks.
But he was young, bold, and active, and, with the assistance of
the begger's stout piked staff, which he retained by advice of
the proprietor, contrived to bear himself from the face of the

precipice, and the yet more hazardous projecting cliffs which varied its surface. Tossed in empty space, like an idle and unsubstantial feather, with a motion that agitated the brain at once with fear and with dizziness, he retained his alertness of exertion and presence of mind; and it was not until he was safely grounded upon the summit of the cliff, that he felt temporary and giddy sickness. As he recovered from a sort of half swoon, he cast his eyes eagerly around. The object which they would most willingly have sought, was already in the act of vanishing. Her white garment was just discernible as she followed on the path which her father had taken. She had lingered till she saw the last of their company rescued from danger, and until she had been assured by the hoarse voice of Mucklebackit, that "the callant had come off wi' unbrizzed banes, and that he was but in a kind of dwam." But Lovel was not aware that she had expressed in his fate even this degree of interest, which, though nothing more than was due to a stranger who had assisted her in such an hour of peril, he would have gladly purchased by braving even more imminent danger than he had that evening been exposed to.

DIANA VERNON.

From the summit of an eminence, I had already had a distant view of Osbaldistone Hall, a large and antiquated edifice,
peeping out from a Druidical grove of huge oaks; and I was
directing my course towards it, as straightly and as speedily as
the windings of a very indifferent road would permit, when my
horse, tired as he was, pricked up his ears at the enlivening notes
of a pack of hounds in full cry, cheered by the occasional bursts
of a French horn, which in those days was the constant accom-
paniment to the chase. I made no doubt that the pack was
my uncle's, and drew up my horse with the purpose of suffering the hunters to pass without notice, aware that a hunting-
field was not the proper scene to introduce myself to a keen sportsman, and determined, when they had passed on, to proceed to
the mansion-house at my own pace, and there to await the return of the proprietor from his sport. I paused, therefore, on
a rising ground, and, not unmoved by the sense of interest which
that species of sylvan sport is so much calculated to inspire,
(although my mind was not at the moment very accessible to

impressions of this nature,) I expected with some eagerness the appearance of the huntsmen.

The fox, hard run, and nearly spent, first made his appearance from the copse which clothed the right hand side of the valley. His drooping brush, his soiled appearance, and jaded trot, proclaimed his fate impending; and the carrion crow, which hovered over him, already considered poor Reynard as soon to be his prey. He crossed the stream which divides the little valley, and was dragging himself up a ravine on the other side of its wild banks, when the headmost hounds, followed by the rest of the pack in full cry, burst from the coppice, followed by the huntsmen, and three or four riders. The dogs pursued the trace of Reynard with unerring instinct; and the hunters followed with reckless haste, regardless of the broken and difficult nature of the ground. They were tall, stout young men, well mounted, and dressed in green and red, the uniform of a sporting association, formed under the auspices of old Sir Hildebrand Osbaldistone. My cousins! thought I, as they swept past me. The next reflection was, what is my reception likely to be among these worthy successors of Nimrod? and how improbable is it that I, knowing little or nothing of rural sports, shall find myself at ease, or happy, in my uncle's family. A vision that passed me interrupted these reflections.

It was a young lady, the loveliness of whose very striking features was enhanced by the animation of the chase and the glow of the exercise, mounted on a beautiful horse, jet-black, unless where he was flecked by spots of the snow-white foam which embossed his bridle. She wore, what was then somewhat unusual, a coat, vest, and hat, resembling those of a man, which fashion has since called a riding habit. The mode had been introduced while I was in France, and was perfectly new to me. Her long black hair streamed on the breeze, having, in the hurry of the chase, escaped from the ribbon which bound it. Some very broken ground, through which she guided her horse with the most admirable address and presence of mind, retarded her course, and brought her closer to me than any of the other riders had passed. I had, therefore, a full view of her uncommonly fine face and person, to which an inexpressible charm was added by the wild gayety of the scene, and the romance of her singular dress and unexpected appearance. As she passed me, her horse made, in his impetuosity, an irregular movement, just while, coming once more upon open ground, she was again putting him to his speed. It served as an apology for me to ride close up to her, as if to her assistance. There was, however, no cause for alarm ; it was not a stumble, nor a false step ; and if it had, the fair Amazon had to much self-possession to have been de-ranged by it. She thanked my good intentions, however, by a smile, and I felt encouraged to put my horse to the same pace, and to keep in her immediate neighborhood. The clamor of " Whoop, dead, dead ! " and the corresponding flour-ish of the French horn, soon announced to us that there was no more occasion for haste, since the chase was at a close. One of the young men whom we had seen, approached us, waving the brush of the fox in triumph, as if to upbraid my fair companion.

" I see," she replied, " I see ; but make no noise about it ; if Phœbe," said she, patting the neck of the beautiful animal on which she rode, " had not got among the cliffs, you would have had little cause for boasting."

They met as she spoke, and I observed them both look at me and converse a moment in an under tone, the young lady apparently pressing the sportsman to do something which he declined shyly, and with a sort of sheepish sullenness. She instantly turned her horse's head towards me, saying—" Well, well, Thornie, if you won't, I must, that's all.—Sir," she continued, addressing me, " I have been endeavoring to persuade this cultivated young gentleman to make inquiry of you, whether, in the course of your travels in these parts, you have heard any thing of a friend of ours, one Mr. Francis Osbaldistone, who has been for some days expected at Osbaldistone Hall ? "

I was too happy to acknowledge myself to be the party inquired after, and to express my thanks for the obliging inquiries of the young lady.

" In that case, sir," she rejoined, " as my kinsman's politeness seems to be still slumbering, you will permit me (though I suppose it is highly improper) to stand mistress of ceremonies, and to present to you young Squire Thorncliff Osbaldistone, your cousin, and Die Vernon, who has also the honor to be your accomplished cousin's poor kinswoman."

There was a mixture of boldness, satire, and simplicity in the manner in which Miss Vernon pronounced these words. My knowledge of life was sufficient to enable me to take up a corresponding tone as I expressed my gratitude to her for her condescension, and my extreme pleasure at having met with them. To say the truth, the compliment was so expressed, that the lady might easily appropriate the greater share of it, for Thorncliff seemed an arrant country bumpkin, awkward, shy, and somewhat sulky withal. He shook hands with me, however, and then intimated his intention of leaving me that he might help the huntsmen and his brothers to couple the hounds, a purpose which he rather communicated by way of information to Miss Vernon than as apology to me.

"There he goes," said the young lady, following him with eyes in which disdain was admirably painted—"the prince of grooms and cock-fighters, and blackguard horse-coursers. But there is not one of them to mend another. Have you read Markham?" said Miss Vernon.

"Read whom, ma'am?—I do not even remember the author's name."

"Oh lud! on what a strand are you wrecked!" replied the young lady. "A poor forlorn and ignorant stranger, unacquainted with the very Alcoran of the savage tribe whom you are come to reside among. Never to have heard of Markham, the most celebrated author on farriery! then I fear you are equally a stranger to the more modern names of Gibson and Bartlett?"

"I am, indeed, Miss Vernon."

"And do you not blush to own it?" said Miss Vernon. "Why, we must forswear your alliance. Then, I suppose you can neither give a ball, nor a mash, nor a horn?"

"I confess I trust all these matters to an hostler or to my groom."

"Incredible carelessness!—And you cannot shoe a horse, or cut his mane and tail; or worm a dog, or crop his ears, or cut his dew claws; or reclaim a hawk, or give him his casting-stones, or direct his diet when he is scaled; or"——

"To sum up my insignificance in one word," replied I, "I am profoundly ignorant in all these rural accomplishments."

"Then, in the name of Heaven, Mr. Francis Osbaldistone,

7

what *can* you do ?   Can you do *this ?*" she said, putting her horse to a canter.

There was a sort of rude overgrown fence crossed the path before us, with a gate, composed of pieces of wood rough from the forest, which I was about to move forward to open, when Miss Vernon cleared the obstruction at a flying leap.   I was bound, in point of honor to follow and was in a moment again at her side.

HELEN MAC-GREGOR.

We approached within about twenty yards of the spot where the advanced guard had seen some appearance of an enemy. It was one of those promontories which run into the lake, and round the base of which the road had hitherto wound in the manner I have described. In the present case, however, the path, instead of keeping the water's edge scaled the promontory by one or two rapid zigzags, carried in a broken track along the precipitous face of a slaty gray rock, which would otherwise have been absolutely inaccessible. On the top of this rock, only to be approached by a road so broken, so narrow, and so precarious, the corporal declared he had seen the bonnets and long-barrelled guns of several mountaineers, apparently couched among the long heath and brushwood which crested the eminence. Captain Thornton ordered him to move forward with three files, to dislodge the supposed ambuscade, while at a more slow but steady pace, he advanced to his support with the rest of his party.

The attack which he meditated was prevented by the unexpected apparition of a female upon the summit of the rock.

"Stand!" she said, with a commanding tone, "and tell me what ye seek in Mac-Gregor's country?"

I have seldom seen a finer or more commanding form than this woman. She might be between the term of forty and fifty years, and had a countenance which must once have been of a masculine cast of beauty; though now, imprinted with deep lines by exposure to rough weather, and perhaps by the wasting influence of grief and passion, its features were only strong, harsh, and expressive. She wore her plaid, not drawn around her head and shoulders, as is the fashion of the women in Scotland, but disposed around her body as the Highland soldiers wear theirs. She had a man's bonnet, with a feather in it, an unsheathed sword in her hand, and a pair of pistols at her girdle.

"It's Helen Campbell, Rob's wife," said the Bailie, in a whisper of considerable alarm; "and there will be broken heads amang us or it's lang."

"What seek ye here?" she asked again of Captain Thornton, who had himself advanced to reconnoitre.

"We seek the outlaw, Rob Roy Mac-Gregor Campbell," answered the officer, "and make no war on women; therefore offer no vain opposition to the king's troops, and assure yourself of civil treatment."

"Ay," retorted the Amazon, "I am no stranger to your tender mercies. Ye have left me neither name nor fame—my mother's bones will shrink aside in their grave when mine are laid beside them.—Ye have left me and mine neither house nor hold, blanket nor bedding, cattle to feed us, or flocks to clothe us.—Ye have taken from us all—all!—The very name of our ancestors have ye taken away, and now ye come for our lives."

"I seek no man's life," replied the captain; "I only exccute my orders. If you are alone, good woman, you have nought to fear—if there are any with you so rash as to offer useless resistance, their own blood be on their own heads. Move forward, sergeant."

The whole advanced with a shout, headed by Captain Thornton, the grenadiers preparing to throw their grenades among the bushes, where the ambuscade lay, and the musketeers to support them by an instant and close assault.

At length, by dint of scrambling, I found a spot which commanded a view of the field of battle. The battle was then ended; and, as my mind augured, from the place and circumstances attending the contest, it had terminated in the defeat of Captain Thornton. I saw a party of Highlanders in the act of disarming that officer, and the scanty remainder of his party. They consisted of about twelve men, most of whom were wounded, who, surrounded by treble their number, and without the power to either advance or retreat, exposed to a murderous and well-aimed fire, which they had no means of returning with effect, had at length laid down their arms by the order of their officer, when he saw that the road in his rear was occupied, and that protracted resistance would be only wasting the lives of his brave followers. By the Highlanders, who fought under cover, the victory was cheaply bought, at the expense of one man slain and two wounded by the grenades.

Leaving Andrew to follow at his leisure, or rather at such leisure as the surrounding crowd were pleased to indulge him with, Dougal hurried us down to the pathway in which the skirmish had been fought, and hastened to present us as additional captives to the female leader of his band.

We were dragged before her accordingly, Dougal fighting, struggling, screaming, as if he were the party most apprehensive of hurt, and repulsing by threats and efforts, all those who attempted to take a nearer interest in our capture than he seemed to do himself. At length we were placed before the heroine of the day, whose appearance, as well as those of the savage, uncouth, yet martial figures who surrounded us, struck me, to own the truth, with considerable apprehension. I do not know if Helen Mac-Gregor had personally mingled in the fray, and indeed I was afterwards given to understand the contrary; but the specks of blood on her brow, her hands, and naked arms, as well as on the blade of the sword which she continued to hold in her hand—her flushed countenance, and the disordered state of the raven locks which escaped from under the red bonnet and plume that formed her head-dress, seemed all to intimate that she had taken an immediate share in the conflict. Her keen black eyes and features expressed an imagination inflamed by the pride of gratified revenge, and the triumph of victory. Yet there was nothing positively sanguinary or cruel in her deportment; and she reminded me, when the immediate alarm of the interview was over, of some of the paintings I had seen of the inspired heroines in the Catholic churches of France.

The lady was about to speak, when a few wild strains of a pibroch were heard advancing up the road from Aberfoil.

The skirmish being of very short duration, the armed men who followed this martial melody, had not, although quickening their march when they heard the firing, been able to arrive in time sufficient to take any share in the reconnoitre. The victory, therefore, was complete without them, and they now arrived only to share in the triumph of their countrymen.

There was a marked difference betwixt the appearance of these new comers and that of the party by which our escort had been defeated, and it was greatly in favor of the former. The thirty or forty Highlanders who now joined the others, were all men in the prime of youth or manhood, active, clean-made fellows, whose short hose and belted plaids set out their sinewy limbs to the best advantage. Their arms were as superior to those of the first party as their dress and appearance.

But it was easy to see that this chosen band had not arrived from a victory such as they found their ill-appointed companions possessed of. The pibroch sent forth occasionally a few wailing notes, expressive of a very different sentiment from triumph; and when they appeared before the wife of their chieftain, it was in silence, and with downcast and melancholy looks. They paused when they approached her, and the pipes again sent forth the same wild and melancholy strain.

Helen rushed towards them with a countenance in which anger was mingled with apprehension. " What means this, Allaster? " she said to the minstrel; " why a lament in the moment of victory?—Robert—Hamish—where's the Mac-Gregor?—where's your father? "

Her sons, who led the band, advanced with slow and irreso-lute steps towards her, and murmured a few words in Gaelic, at hearing which she set up a shriek that made the rocks ring again, in which all the women and boys joined, clapping their hands and yelling, as if their lives had been expiring in the sound.

" Taken ! " repeated Helen, when the clamor had subsided— " Taken !—captive !—and you live to say so ? Coward dogs ! did I nurse you for this, that you should spare your blood on your father's enemies ? or see him prisoner, and come back to tell it ? "

At length, when her resentment appeared in some degree

to subside, the eldest son, speaking in English, probably that
he might not be understood by their followers, endeavored re-
spectfully to vindicate himself and his brother from his mother's
reproaches.   I was so near him as to comprehend much of what
he said ; and, as it was of great consequence to me to be possessed of information in this great crisis, I failed not to listen as
attentively as I could.

" The Mac-Gregor," his son stated, " had been called out
upon a trysting with a Lowland hallion, who came with a token
from "—he muttered the name very low, but I thought it
sounded like my own.—" The Mac-Gregor," he said, " accepted
of the invitation, but commanded the Saxon who brought the
message to be detained, as a hostage that good faith should be
observed to him.   Accordingly he went to the place of appoint-
ment," (which had some wild Highland name that I cannot remember,) " attended only by Angus Breck and little Rory, commanding no one to follow him.   Within half an hour Angus
Breck came back with the doleful tidings that the Mac-Gregor
had been surprised and made prisoner by a party of Lennox
militia, under Galbraith of Garschattachin."

Under the burning influence of the thirst for vengeance, the
wife of Mac-Gregor commanded that the hostage exchanged for
his safety should be brought into her presence.   I believe her
sons had kept this unfortunate wretch out of her sight, for fear
of the consequences ; but if it was so, their humane precaution
only postponed his fate.   They dragged forward, at her summons,
a wretch already half dead with terror, in whose agonized features I recognized, to my horror and astonishment, my old acquaintance Morris.

He fell prostrate before the female chief with an effort to
clasp her knees, from which she drew back, as if his touch had

been pollution, so that all he could do in token of the extremity of his humiliation, was to kiss the hem of her plaid. I never heard entreaties for life poured forth with such agony of spirit. The ecstasy of fear was such, that, instead of paralyzing his tongue, as on ordinary occasions, it even rendered him eloquent; and, with cheeks pale as ashes, hands compressed in agony, eyes that seemed to be taking their last look of all mortal objects, he protested, with the deepest oaths, his total ignorance of any design on the person of Rob Roy, whom he swore he loved and honored as his own soul. In the inconsistency of his terror, he said he was but the agent of others, and he muttered the name of Rashleigh. He prayed but for life—for life he would give all he had in the world: it was but life he asked—life, if it were to be prolonged under tortures and privations: he asked only breath, though it should be drawn in the damps of the lowest caverns of their hills.

It is impossible to describe the scorn, the loathing, and contempt, with which the wife of Mac-Gregor regarded this wretched petitioner for the poor boon of existence.

"I could have bid you live," she said, "had life been to you the same weary and wasting burden that it is to me—that it is to every noble and generous mind. But you—wretch! you could creep through the world unaffected by its various disgraces, its ineffable miseries, its constantly accumulating masses of crime and sorrow: you could live and enjoy yourself, while the noble-minded are betrayed—while nameless and birthless villains tread on the neck of the brave and the long-descended: you could enjoy yourself, like a butcher's dog in the shambles, battening on garbage, while the slaughter of the oldest and best went on around you! This enjoyment you shall not live to partake of; you shall die, base dog, and that before yon cloud has passed over the sun."

8

She gave a brief command in Gaelic to her attendants, two of whom seized upon the prostrate supplicant, and hurried him to the brink of a cliff which overhung the flood.   He set up the most piercing and dreadful cries that fear ever uttered—I may well term them dreadful, for they haunted my sleep for years afterwards.   As the murderers, or executioners—call them as you will—dragged him along, he recognized me even in that moment of horror, and exclaimed, in the last articulate words I ever heard him utter, " Oh, Mr. Osbaldistone, save me!— save me ! "

I was so much moved by this horrid spectacle, that, although in momentary expectation of sharing his fate, I did attempt to speak in his behalf ; but, as might have been expected, my inter- ference was sternly disregarded.   The victim was held fast by some, while others, binding a large heavy stone in a plaid, tied it round his neck, and others again eagerly stripped him of some part of his dress.   Half-naked, and thus manacled, they hurled him into the lake, there about twelve feet deep, with a loud halloo of vindictive triumph, above which, however, his last death- shriek, the yell of mortal agony, was distinctly heard.   The heavy burden splashed in the dark-blue waters, and the High- landers, with their pole-axes and swords, watched an instant, to guard, lest, extricating himself from the load to which he was attached, the victim might have struggled to regain the shore. But the knot had been securely bound ; the wretched man sunk without effort ; the waters, which his fall had disturbed, settled calmly over him, and the unit of that life for which he had pleaded so strongly, was forever withdrawn from the sum of human existence.

ISABELLA VERE.

He brings Earl Osmond to receive my vows.
O dreadful change! for Tancred, haughty Osmond.
Tancred and Sigismunda.

Mr. Vere, whom long practice of dissimulation had enabled
to model his very gait and footsteps to aid the purposes of de-
ception, walked along the stone passage, and up the first flight
of steps towards Miss Vere's apartment, with the alert, firm, and
steady pace of one, who is bound, indeed, upon important
business, but who entertains no doubt he can terminate his af-
fairs satisfactorily.   But when out of hearing of the gentlemen
whom he had left, his step became so slow and irresolute, as to
correspond with his doubts and his fears.   At length he paused
in an antechamber to collect his ideas, and form his plan of argument, before approaching his daughter.

"In what more hopeless and inextricable dilemma was ever
an unfortunate man involved!"—Such was the tenor of his reflections.—"If we now fall to pieces by disunion, there can be
little doubt that the government will take my life as the prime
agitator of the insurrection.   Or, grant I could stoop to save
myself by a hasty submission, am I not, even in that case, utterly

ruined? I have broken irreconcilably with Ratcliffe, and can
have nothing to expect from that quarter but insult and persecu-
tion. I must wander forth an impoverished and dishonored
man, without even the means of sustaining life, far less wealth
sufficient to counterbalance the infamy which my countrymen,
both those whom I desert and those whom I join, will attach to
the name of the political renegade. It is not to be thought of.
And yet, what choice remains between this lot and the igno-
minious scaffold? Nothing can save me but reconciliation with
these men; and, to accomplish this, I have promised to Langley
that Isabella shall marry him ere midnight, and to Mareschal,
that she shall do so without compulsion. I have but one remedy
betwixt me and ruin—her consent to take a suitor whom she
dislikes, upon such short notice as would disgust her, even were
he a favored lover.—But I must trust to the romantic generosity of her disposition; and let me paint the necessity of her
obedience ever so strongly, I cannot overcharge its reality."

Having finished this sad chain of reflections upon his perilous condition, he entered his daughter's apartment with every
nerve bent up to the support of the argument which he was
about to sustain. Though a deceitful and ambitious man, he
was not so devoid of natural affection but that he was shocked
at the part he was about to act, in practising on the feelings of
a dutiful and affectionate child; but the recollections, that, if
he succeeded, his daughter would only be trepanned into an ad-
vantageous match, and that, if he failed, he himself was a lost
man, were quite sufficient to drown all scruples.

He found Miss Vere seated by the window of her dressing-
room, her head reclining on her hand, and either sunk in slumber, or so deeply engaged in meditation, that she did not hear
the noise he made at his entrance. He approached with his

features composed to a deep expression of sorrow and sympathy, and, sitting down beside her, solicited her attention by quietly taking her hand, a motion which he did not fail to accompany with a deep sigh.

"My father!" said Isabella, with a sort of start, which expressed at least as much fear, as joy or affection.

"Yes, Isabella," said Vere, "your unhappy father, who comes now as a penitent to crave forgiveness of his daughter for an injury done to her in the excess of his affection, and then to take leave of her forever."

"Sir? Offence to me? Take leave forever? What does all this mean?" said Miss Vere.

"Yes, Isabella, I am serious. But first let me ask you, have you no suspicion that I may have been privy to the strange chance which befell you yesterday morning?"

"You, sir?" answered Isabella, stammering between a consciousness that he had guessed her thoughts justly, and the shame as well as fear which forbade her to acknowledge a suspicion so degrading and so unnatural.

"Yes!" he continued, "your hesitation confesses that you entertained such an opinion, and I have now the painful task of acknowledging that your suspicions have done me no injustice. But listen to my motives. In an evil hour I countenanced the-addresses of Sir Frederick Langley, conceiving it impossible that you could have any permanent objections to a match where the advantages were, in most respects, on your side. In a word, I entered with him into measures calculated to restore our banished monarch and the independence of my country. He has taken advantage of my unguarded confidence, and now has my life at his disposal."

"Your life, sir?" said Isabella, faintly.

"Yes, Isabella," continued her father, "the life of him who gave life to you. So soon as I foresaw the excesses into which his headlong passion (for to do him justice, I believe his unreasonable conduct arises from excess of attachment to you) was likely to hurry him, I endeavored, by finding a plausible pretext for your absence for some weeks, to extricate myself from the dilemma in which I am placed. For this purpose I wished, in case your objections to the match continued insurmountable, to have sent you privately for a few months to the convent of your maternal aunt at Paris. By a series of mistakes you have been brought from the place of secrecy and security which I had destined for your temporary abode. Fate has baffled my last chance of escape, and I have only to give you my blessing, and send you from the castle with Mr. Ratcliffe, who now leaves it; my own fate will soon be decided."

"Good Heaven, sir! can this be possible?" exclaimed Isabella. "Oh, why was I freed from the restraint in which you placed me? or why did you not impart your pleasure to me?"

"Think an instant, Isabella. Would you have had me prejudice in your opinion the friend I was most desirous of serving, by communicating to you the injurious eagerness with which he pursued his object? Could I do so honorably, having promised to assist his suit?—But it is all over. I and Mareschal have made up our minds to die like men; it only remains to send you from hence under a safe escort."

"Great powers! and is there no remedy?" said the terrified young woman.

"None, my child," answered Vere, gently, "unless one which you would not advise your father to adopt—to be the first to betray his friends."

"Oh, no! no!" she answered, abhorrently yet hastily, as if

to reject the temptation which the alternative presented to her. "But is there no other hope—through flight—through mediation—through supplication?—I will bend my knee to Sir Frederick!"

"It would be a fruitless degradation; he is determined on his course, and I am equally resolved to stand the hazard of my fate. On one condition only he will turn aside from his purpose, and that condition my lips shall never utter to you."

"Name it, I conjure you, my dear father!" exclaimed Isabella. "What *can* he ask that we ought not to grant, to prevent the hideous catastrophe with which you are threatened?"

"That, Isabella," said Vere, solemnly, "you shall never know, until your father's head has rolled on the bloody scaffold; then, indeed, you will learn there was one sacrifice by which he might have been saved."

"And why not speak it now?" said Isabella; "do you fear I would flinch from the sacrifice of fortune for your preservation? or would you bequeath me the bitter legacy of life-long remorse, so oft as I shall think that you perished, while there remained one mode of preventing the dreadful misfortune that overhangs you?"

"Then, my child," said Vere, "since you press me to name what I would a thousand times rather leave in silence, I must inform you that he will accept for ransom nothing but your hand in marriage, and that conferred before midnight this very evening!"

"This evening, sir?" said the young lady, struck with horror at the proposal—"and to such a man!—A man?—a monster, who could wish to win the daughter by threatening the life of the father—it is impossible!"

"You say right, my child," answered her father, "it is indeed impossible; nor have I either the right or the wish to exact such a sacrifice.—It is the course of nature that the old should die and be forgot, and the young should live and be happy."

"My father die, and his child can save him!—but no—no —my dear father, pardon me, it is impossible, you only wish to guide me to your wishes. I know your object is what you think my happiness, and this dreadful tale is only told, to influence my conduct and subdue my scruples."

"My daughter," replied Ellieslaw, in a tone where offended authority seemed to struggle with parental affection, " my child suspects me of inventing a false tale to work upon her feelings! Even this I must bear, and even from this unworthy suspicion I must descend to vindicate myself. You know the stainless honor of your cousin Mareschal—mark what I shall write to him, and judge from his answer, if the danger in which we stand is not real, and whether I have not used every means to avert it."

He sat down, wrote a few lines hastily, and handed them to Isabella, who, after repeated and painful efforts, cleared her eyes and head sufficiently to discern their purport.

"Dear cousin," said the billet, " I find my daughter, as I expected, in despair at the untimely and premature urgency of Sir Frederick Langley. She cannot even comprehend the peril in which we stand, or how much we are in his power. Use your influence with him, for Heaven's sake, to modify proposals, to the acceptance of which I cannot, and will not, urge my child against all her own feelings, as well as those of delicacy and propriety, and oblige your loving cousin,—R. V."

In the agitation of the moment, when her swimming eyes and dizzy brain could hardly comprehend the sense of what she looked upon, it is not surprising that Miss Vere should have omitted to remark that this letter seemed to rest her scruples rather upon the form and time of the proposed union, than on a rooted dislike to the suitor proposed to her. Mr. Vere rang the bell, and gave the letter to a servant to be delivered to Mr. Mareschal, and, rising from his chair, continued to traverse the apartment in silence and in great agitation until the answer was returned. He glanced it over, and wrung the hand of his daughter as he gave it to her. The tenor was as follows :—

" My dear kinsman, I have already urged the knight on the point you mention, and I find him as fixed as Cheviot. I am truly sorry my fair cousin should be pressed to give up any of her maidenly rights. Sir Frederick consents, however, to leave the castle with me the instant the ceremony is performed, and we will raise our followers and begin the fray. Thus there is great hope the bridegroom may be knocked on the head before he and the bride can meet again, so Bell has a fair chance to be Lady Langley à très bon marché. For the rest, I can only say, that if she can make up her mind to the alliance at all—it is no time for mere maiden ceremony—my pretty cousin must needs consent to marry in haste, or we shall all repent at leisure, or rather have very little leisure to repent ; which is all at present from him who rests your affectionate kinsman,—R. M."

" P. S. Tell Isabella that I would rather cut the knight's throat after all, and end the dilemma that way, than see her constrained to marry him against her will."

When Miss Vere had read this letter, she became deadly pale, clenched her hands, pressing the palms strongly together, closed her eyes, and drew her lips with strong compression, as if the severe constraint which she put upon her internal feelings extended even to her muscular organization. Then raising her head, and drawing in her breath strongly ere she spoke, she said, with firmness,—" Father, I consent to the marriage."

9

" You shall not—you shall not—my child—my dear child—
you shall not embrace certain misery to free me from uncertain
danger."

So exclaimed Ellieslaw; and, strange and inconsistent beings that we are! he expressed the real though momentary
feelings of his heart.

" Father," repeated Isabella, " I will consent to this marriage."

" No, my child, no—not now at least—we will humble ourselves to obtain delay from him; and yet, Isabella, could you
overcome a dislike which has no real foundation, think, in other
respects, what a match !—wealth—rank—importance."

" Father ! " reiterated Isabella, " I have consented."

It seemed as if she had lost the power of saying any thing
else, or even of varying the phrase which, with such efforts, she
had compelled herself to utter.

" Forgive me, my child—I go—Heaven bless thee.   At
eleven—if you call me not before—I will come to seek you."

When he left Isabella she dropped upon her knees.—" Heaven
aid me to support the resolution I have taken.—Heaven only
can.—Oh, poor Earnscliff ! who shall comfort him ? and with
what contempt will he pronounce her name, who listened to him
to-day and gave herself to another at night !   But let him despise me—better so than that he should know the truth.—Let
him despise me ; if it will but lessen his grief, I should feel comfort in the loss of his esteem."

She wept bitterly ; attempting in vain, from time to time,
to commence the prayer for which she had sunk on her knees,
but unable to calm her spirits sufficiently for the exercise of devotion.   As she remained in this agony of mind, the door of her
apartment was slowly opened.

JENNY DENNISON.

WHILE Lady Margaret held, with the high-descended sergeant of dragoons, the conference which we have detailed in the preceding pages, her grand-daughter, partaking in a less degree her ladyship's enthusiasm for all who were sprung of the blood-royal, did not honor Sergeant Bothwell with more attention than a single glance, which showed her a tall, powerful person, and a set of hardy, weatherbeaten features, to which pride and dissipation had given an air where discontent mingled with the reckless gayety of desperation. The other soldiers offered still less to detach her consideration; but from the prisoner, muffled and disguised as he was, she found it impossible to withdraw her eyes. Yet she blamed herself for indulging a curiosity which seemed obviously to give pain to him who was its object.

"I wish," she said to Jenny Dennison, who was the immediate attendant on her person—"I wish we knew who that poor fellow is."

"I was just thinking sae mysell, Miss Edith," said the waiting woman, "but it canna be Cuddie Headrigg, because he's taller and no sae stout."

"Yet," continued Miss Bellenden, "it may be some poor

neighbor, for whom we might have cause to interest ourselves."

" I can sune learn wha he is," said the enterprising Jenny, " if the sodgers were anes settled and at leisure, for I ken ane o' them very weel—the best-looking and the youngest o' them."

" I think you know all the idle young fellows about the country," answered her mistress.

" Na, Miss Edith, I am no sae free o' my acquaintance as that," answered the fille-de-chambre. " To be sure, folk canna help kenning the folk by headmark that they see aye glowring and looking at them at kirk and market; but I ken few lads to speak to unless it be them o' the family, and the three Steinsons, and Tam Rand, and the young miller, and the five Howisons in Nethersheils, and lang Tam Gilry, and "——

" Pray cut short a list of exceptions which threatens to be a long one, and tell me how you come to know this young soldier," said Miss Bellenden.

" Lord, Miss Edith, it's Tam Halliday, Trooper Tam, as they ca' him, that was wounded by the hill-folk at the conventicle at Outer-side Muir, and lay here while he was under cure. I can ask him ony thing, and Tam will no refuse to answer me, I'll be caution for him."

" Try, then," said Miss Edith, " if you can find an opportunity to ask him the name of his prisoner, and come to my room and tell me what he says."

Jenny Dennison proceeded on her errand, but soon returned with such a face of surprise and dismay as evinced a deep interest in the fate of the prisoner.

" What is the matter ? " said Edith, anxiously ; " does it prove to be Cuddie, after all, poor fellow ? "

" Cuddie, Miss Edith ? Na ! na ! it's nae Cuddie," blub-

bered out the faithful fille-de-chambre, sensible of the pain
which her news was about to inflict on her young mistress.
" Oh dear, Miss Edith, it's young Milnwood himsell ! "

" Young Milnwood ! " exclaimed Edith, aghast in her turn ;
" it is impossible—totally impossible !—His uncle attends the
clergyman indulged by law, and has no connection whatever
with the refractory people ; and he himself has never interfered
in this unhappy dissension ; he must be totally innocent, unless
he has been standing up for some invaded right."

" Oh, my dear Miss Edith," said her attendant, ." these are
not days to ask what's right or what's wrang ; if he were as innocent as the new-born infant, they would find some way of
making him guilty, if they liked ; but Tam Halliday says it will
touch his life, for he has been resetting ane o' the Fife gentlemen that killed that auld carle of an Archbishop."

" His life ! " exclaimed Edith, starting hastily up, and speaking with a hurried and tremulous accent,—" they cannot—they
shall not—I will speak for him—they shall not hurt him ! "

" Oh, my dear young leddy, think on your grandmother ;
think on the danger and the difficulty," added Jenny ; " for he's
kept under close confinement till Claverhouse comes up in the
morning, and if he doesna gie him full satisfaction, Tam Halliday says there will be brief wark wi' him.—Kneel down—mak
ready—present—fire—just as they did wi' auld deaf John Mac-
briar, that never understood a single question they pat till him,
and sae lost his life for lack o' hearing."

" Jenny," said the young lady, " if he should die, I will die
with him ; there is no time to talk of danger or difficulty.—I
will put on a plaid, and slip down with you to the place where
they have kept him.—I will throw myself at the feet of the sentinel, and entreat him, as he has a soul to be saved,"——

"Eh! guide us," interrupted the maid, "our young leddy at the feet o' Trooper Tam, and speaking to him about his soul, when the puir chield hardly kens whether he has ane or no, unless that he whiles swears by it—that will never do; but what maun be maun be, and I'll never desert a true love cause.—And sae, if ye maun see young Milnwood, though I ken no gude it will do, but to make baith your hearts the sairer, I'll e'en tak the risk o't, and try to manage Tam Halliday; but ye maun let me hae my ain gate and no speak ae word—he's keeping guard o'er Milnwood in the easter round of the tower."

"Go, go, fetch me a plaid," said Edith. "Let me but see him, and I will find some remedy for his danger.—Haste ye, Jenny, as ever ye hope to have good at my hands."

Jenny hastened, and soon returned with a plaid, in which Edith muffled herself so as in part to disguise her person. This was a mode of arranging the plaid very common among the ladies of that century, and the earlier part of the succeeding one; so much so, indeed, that the venerable sages of the Kirk, conceiving that the mode gave tempting facilities for intrigue, directed more than one act of Assembly against this use of the mantle. But fashion, as usual, proved too strong for authority, and while plaids continued to be worn, women of all ranks occasionally employed them as a sort of muffler or veil. Her face and figure thus concealed, Edith, holding by her attendant's arm, hastened with trembling steps to the place of Morton's confinement.

This was a small study or closet, in one of the turrets, opening upon a gallery in which the sentinel was pacing to and fro; for Sergeant Bothwell, scrupulous in observing his word, and perhaps touched with some compassion for the prisoner's youth and genteel demeanor, had waived the indignity of putting his guard into the same apartment with him. Halliday, therefore, with his carbine on his arm, walked up and down the gallery, occasionally solacing himself with a draught of ale, a huge flagon of which stood upon a table at one end of the apartment, and at other times humming the lively Scottish air,

> " Between Saint Johnstone and Bonny Dundee,
> I'll gar ye be fain to follow me."

Jenny Dennison cautioned her mistress once more to let her take her own way.

"I can manage the trooper weel eneugh," she said; "for as rough as he is, I ken their nature weel; but ye maunna say a single word."

She accordingly opened the door of the gallery just as the sentinel had turned his back from it, and taking up the tune which he hummed, she sung in a coquettish tone of rustic raillery,

> " If I were to follow a poor sodger lad,
> My friends wad be angry, my minnie be mad;
> A laird, or a lord, they were fitter for me,
> Sae I'll never be fain to follow thee."——

" A fair challenge, by Jove," cried the sentinel turning round, "and from two at once; but it's not easy to bang the soldier with his bandoleers;" then taking up the song where the damsel had stopped

> " To follow me ye weel may be glad,
> A share of my supper, a share of my bed,
> To the sound of the drum to range fearless and free,
> I'll gar ye be fain to follow me."——

" Come, my pretty lass, and kiss me for my song."

"I should not have thought of that, Mr. Halliday," answered Jenny, with a look and tone expressing just the necessary degree of contempt at the proposal, "and I'se assure ye, ye'll hae but little o' my company unless ye show gentler havings.— It wasna to hear that sort o' nonsense that brought me here wi' my friend, and ye should think shame o' yoursell, 'at should ye."

" Umph! and what sort of nonsense did bring you here then, Mrs. Dennison?"

"My kinswoman has some particular business with your prisoner, young Mr. Harry Morton, and I am come wi' her to speak till him."

"The devil you are!" answered the sentinel; "and pray, Mrs. Dennison, how do your kinswoman and you propose to get in? You are rather too plump to whisk through a keyhole, and opening the door is a thing not to be spoken of."

" It's no a thing to be spoken o', but a thing to be dune," replied the persevering damsel.

" We'll see about that, my bonny Jenny;" and the soldier resumed his march, humming, as he walked to and fro along the gallery,

> "Keek into the draw-well,
>   Janet, Janet,
>   Then ye'll see your bonny sell,
>   My joe Janet."

"So ye're no thinking to let us in, Mr. Halliday? Weel, weel; gude e'en to you—ye hae seen the last o' me, and o' this bonny die too," said Jenny, holding between her finger and thumb a splendid silver dollar.

" Give him gold, give him gold," whispered the agitated young lady.

" Silver's e'en ower gude for the like o' him," replied Jenny,

" that disna care for the blink o' a bonny lassie's ee—and what's waur, he wad think there was something mair in't than a kins- woman o' mine. My certy! siller's no sae plenty wi' us, let alane gowd." Having addressed this advice aside to her mis- tress, she raised her voice, and said, " My cousin winna stay ony langer, Mr. Halliday; sae, if ye please, gude e'en t'ye."

" Halt a bit, halt a bit," said the trooper; " rein up and parley, Jenny. If I let your kinswoman in to speak to my prisoner, you may stay here and keep me company till she come out again, and then we'll all be well pleased you know."

" The fiend be in my feet then," said Jenny; " d'ye think my kinswoman and me are gaun to lose our gude name wi' cracking clavers wi' the likes o' you or your prisoner either, with- out somebody by to see fair play? Heigh, heigh, sirs, to see sic a difference between folk's promises and performances! ye were aye willing to slight puir Cuddie; but an I had asked him to oblige me in a thing, though it had been to cost his hanging, he wadna hae stude twice about it."

" D—n Cuddie ! " retorted the dragoon, " he'll be hanged in good earnest, I hope. I saw him to-day at Milnwood with his old puritanical mother, and if I had thought I was to have had him cast in my dish, I would have brought him up at my horse's tail—we had law enough to bear us out."

" Very weel, very weel.—See if Cuddie winna hae a lang shot at you ane o' thae days, if ye gar him tak the muir wi' sae mony honest folk. He can hit a mark brawly; he was third at the popinjay; and he's as true of his promise as of ee and hand, though he disna mak sic a phrase about it as some acquaint- ance o' yours.—But it's a' ane to me.—Come, cousin, we'll awa'."

" Stay, Jenny ; d—n me, if I hang fire more than another
10

when I have said a thing," said the soldier, in a hesitating tone. " Where is the sergeant ? "

" Drinking and driving ower," quoth Jenny, " wi' the Steward and John Gudyill."

" So, so—he's safe enough—and where are my comrades ? " asked Halliday.

" Birling the brown bowl wi' the fowler and the falconer, and some o' the serving folk."

" Have they plenty of ale ? "

" Sax gallons, as gude as e'er was masked," said the maid.

" Well, then, my pretty Jenny," said the relenting sentinel, " they are fast till the hour of relieving guard, and perhaps something later ; and so, if you will promise to come alone the next time "——

" Maybe I will, and maybe I winna," said Jenny ; " but if ye get the dollar, ye'll like that just as weel."

" And if I were trusting to you, you little jilting devil, I should lose both pains and powder; whereas this fellow," looking at the piece, " will be good as far as he goes. So, come, there is the door open for you ; do not stay groaning and praying with the young whig now, but be ready, when I call at the door, to start, as if they were sounding ' Horse and away.' "

So speaking, Halliday unlocked the door of the closet, admitted Jenny and her pretended kinswoman, locked it behind them, and hastily reassumed the indifferent measured step and time-killing whistle of a sentinel upon his regular duty.

EDITH BELLENDEN.

The door, which slowly opened, discovered Morton with both arms reclined upon a table, and his head resting upon them in a posture of deep dejection. He raised his face as the door opened, and, perceiving the female figures which it admitted, started up in great surprise. Edith, as if modesty had quelled the courage which despair had bestowed, stood about a yard from the door without having either the power to speak or to advance. All the plans of aid, relief, or comfort, which she had proposed to lay before her lover, seemed at once to have vanished from her recollection, and left only a painful chaos of ideas, with which was mingled a fear that she had degraded herself in the eyes of Morton, by a step which might appear precipitate and unfeminine. ⁻She hung motionless and almost powerless upon the arm of her attendant, who in vain endeavored to reassure and inspire her with courage, by whispering, " We are in now, madam, and we maun mak the best o' our time ; for, doubtless, the corporal or the sergeant will gang the rounds, and it wad be a pity to hae the poor lad Halliday punished for his civility."

Morton, in the mean time, was timidly advancing, suspecting the truth ; for what other female in the house, excepting Edith

herself, was likely to take an interest in his misfortunes; and
yet afraid, owing to the doubtful twilight and muffled dress, of
making some mistake which might be prejudicial to the object
of his affections.   Jenny, whose ready wit and forward manners
well qualified her for such an office, hastened to break the ice.

"Mr. Morton, Miss Edith's very sorry for your present
situation, and"——

It was needless to say more; he was at her side, almost at
her feet, pressing her unresisting hands, and loading her with a
profusion of thanks, and gratitude which would be hardly intelligible, from the mere broken words, unless we could describe
the tone, the gesture, the impassioned and hurried indications
of deep and tumultuous feeling, with which they were accompanied.

For two or three minutes, Edith stood as motionless as the
statue of a saint which receives the adoration of a worshipper;
and when she recovered herself sufficiently to withdraw her
hands from Henry's grasp, she could at first only faintly articulate, "I have taken a strange step, Mr. Morton—a step," she
continued, with more coherence, as her ideas arranged themselves in consequence of a strong effort, "that perhaps may ex-
pose me to censure in your eyes.   But I have long permitted
you to use the language of friendship—perhaps I might say
more—too long to leave you when the world seems to have left
you.   How, or why, is this imprisonment? what can be done?
can my uncle, who thinks so highly of you—can your own kinsman, Milnwood, be of no use? are there no means? and what
is likely to be the event?"

"Be what it will," answered Henry, contriving to make
himself master of the hand that had escaped from him, but
which was now again abandoned to his clasp, "be what it

will, it is to me from this moment the most welcome incident
of a weary life. To you, dearest Edith—forgive me, I should
have said Miss Bellenden, but misfortune claims strange privi-
leges—to you I have owed the few happy moments which have
gilded a gloomy existence ; and if I am now to lay it down, the
recollection of this honor will be my happiness in the last hour
of suffering."

" But is it even thus, Mr. Morton ? " said Miss Bellenden.
" Have you, who used to mix so little in these unhappy feuds,
become so suddenly and deeply implicated, that nothing short
of "—

She paused, unable to bring out the word which should
have come next.

" Nothing short of my life, you would say ? " replied Morton, in a calm but melancholy tone ; " I believe that will be entirely in the bosoms of my judges. My guards spoke of a possibility of exchanging the penalty for entry into foreign service.
I thought I could have embraced the alternative ; and yet, Miss
Bellenden, since I have seen you once more, I feel that exile
would be more galling than death."

" And is it then true," said Edith, " that you have been so
desperately rash as to entertain communication with any of those
cruel wretches who assassinated the primate ? "

" I knew not even that such a crime had been committed,"
replied Morton, " when I gave unhappily a night's lodging and
concealment to one of those rash and cruel men, the ancient
friend and comrade of my father. But my ignorance will avail
me little ; for who, Miss Bellenden, save you, will believe it ?
And, what is worse, I am at least uncertain whether, even if I
had known the crime, I could have brought my mind, under all
the circumstances, to refuse a temporary refuge to the fugitive."

"And by whom," said Edith, anxiously, "or under what authority, will the investigation of your conduct take place?"

"Under that of Colonel Grahame of Claverhouse, I am given to understand," said Morton; "one of the military commission, to whom it has pleased our king, our privy council, and our parliament, that used to be more tenacious of our liberties, to commit the sole charge of our goods and of our lives."

"You are lost—you are lost, if you are to plead your cause with Claverhouse!" sighed Edith; "root and branchwork is the mildest of his expressions. The unhappy primate was his intimate friend and early patron. 'No excuse, no subterfuge,' said his letter, 'shall save either those connected with the deed, or such as have given them countenance and shelter, from the ample and bitter penalty of the law, until I shall have taken as many lives in vengeance of this atrocious murder as the old man had gray hairs upon his venerable head.' There is neither ruth nor favor to be found with him."

Jenny Dennison, who had hitherto remained silent, now ventured, in the extremity of distress which the lovers felt, but for which they were unable to devise a remedy, to offer her own advice.

"Wi' your leddyship's pardon, Miss Edith, and young Mr. Morton's, we maunna waste time. Let Milnwood take my plaid and gown; I'll slip them aff in the dark corner, if he'll promise no to look about, and he may walk past Tam Halliday, who is half blind with his ale, and I can tell him a canny way to get out o' the Tower, and your leddyship will gang quietly to your ain room, and I'll row mysell in his gray cloak, and pit on his hat, and play the prisoner till the coast's clear, and then I'll cry in Tam Halliday, and gar him let me out."

"Let you out?" said Morton; "they'll make your life answer it."

"Ne'er a bit," replied Jenny; "Tam daurna tell he let ony body in, for his ain sake: and I'll gar him find some other gate to account for the escape."

"Will you, by G—?" said the sentinel, suddenly opening the door of the apartment; "if I am half blind, I am not deaf, and you should not plan an escape quite so loud, if you expect to go through with it. Come, come, Mrs. Janet—march, troop —quick time—trot, d—n me! And you, madam kinswoman —I won't ask your real name, though you were going to play me so rascally a trick—but I must make a clear garrison; so beat a retreat, unless you would have me turn out the guard."

"I hope," said Morton, very anxiously, "you will not mention this circumstance, my good friend, and trust to my honor to acknowledge your civility in keeping the secret. If you overheard our conversation, you must have observed that we did not accept of, or enter into, the hasty proposal made by this good-natured girl."

"Oh, devilish good-natured, to be sure," said Halliday. "As for the rest, I guess how it is, and I scorn to bear malice, or tell tales, as much as another; but no thanks to that little jilting devil, Jenny Dennison, who deserves a tight skelping for trying to lead an honest lad into a scrape, just because he was so silly as to like her good-for-little chit face."

Jenny had no better means of justification than the last apology to which her sex trust, and usually not in vain; she pressed her handkerchief to her face, sobbed with great vehemence, and either wept, or managed, as Halliday might have said, to go through the motions wonderfully well.

"And now," continued the soldier, somewhat mollified, "if

you have any thing to say, say it in two minutes, and let me see your backs turned; for if Bothwell take it into his drunken head to make the rounds half an hour too soon, it will be a black business to us all."

"Farewell, Edith," whispered Morton, assuming a firmness he was far from possessing; "do not remain here—leave me to my fate—it cannot be beyond endurance, since you are interested in it. Good night, good night! Do not remain here till you are discovered."

Thus saying, he resigned her to her attendant, by whom she was partly led and partly supported out of the apartment.

"Every one has his taste, to be sure," said Halliday; "but d—n me if I would have vexed so sweet a girl as that is, for all the whigs that ever swore the Covenant."

JEANIE DEANS.

SHE was short, and rather too stoutly made for her size, had gray eyes, light-colored hair, a round good-humored face, much tanned with the sun, and her only peculiar charm was an air of inexpressible serenity, which a good conscience, kind feelings, contented temper, and the regular discharge of all her duties, spread over her features. There was nothing, it may be supposed, very appalling in the form or manners of this rustic heroine.

"Reuben," she said, at once, " I am bound on a lang journey—I am gaun to Lunnon to ask Effie's life of the king and of the queen."

" Jeanie ! you are surely not yourself," answered Butler, in the utmost surprise ; *you* go to London—*you* address the king and queen ! "

" And what for no, Reuben ? " said Jeanie, with all the composed simplicity of her character ; " it's but speaking to a mortal man and woman when a' is done. And their hearts maun be made o' flesh and blood like other folk's, and Effie's story wad melt them were they stane. Forby, I hae heard that they are no sic bad folk as what the jacobites ca' them."

" Yes, Jeanie," said Butler ; " but their magnificence—their retinue—the difficulty of getting audience ? "

11

"I have thought of a' that, Reuben, and it shall not break my spirit. Nae doubt their claiths will be very grand, wi' their crowns on their heads, and their sceptres in their hands, like the great King Ahasuerus when he sate upon his royal throne foranent the gate of his house, as we are told in Scripture. But I have that within me that will keep my heart from failing, and I am amaist sure that I will be strengthened to speak the errand I came for."

"Alas! alas!" said Butler, "the kings now-a-days do not sit in the gate to administer justice, as in patriarchal times. I know as little of courts as you do, Jeanie, by experience; but by reading and report I know, that the King of Britain does every thing by means of his ministers."

"And if they be upright, God-fearing ministers," said Jeanie, "it's sae muckle the better chance for Effie and me."

"But you do not even understand the most ordinary words relating to a court," said Butler; "by the ministry is meant not clergymen, but the king's official servants."

"Nae doubt," returned Jeanie, "he maun hae a great number mair, I daur to say, than the Duchess has at Dalkeith, and great folk's servants are aye mair saucy than themselves. But I'll be decently put on, and I'll offer them a trifle o' siller, as if I came to see the palace. Or, if they scruple that, I'll tell them I'm come on a business of life and death, and then they will surely bring me to speech of the king and queen."

Butler shook his head. "Oh Jeanie, this is entirely a wild dream. You can never see them but through some great lord's intercession, and I think it is scarce possible even then."

"Weel, but maybe I can get that too," said Jeanie, "with a little helping from you."

"From me, Jeanie, this is the wildest imagination of all."

"Aye, but it is not, Reuben. Havena I heard you say that your grandfather (that my father never likes to hear about) did some gude langsyne to the forbear of this Mac-Callummore, when he was Lord of Lorn?"

"He did so," said Butler, eagerly, "and I can prove it—I will write to the Duke of Argyle—report speaks him a good kindly man, as he is known for a brave soldier and true patriot —I will conjure him to stand between your sister and this cruel fate. There is but a poor chance of success, but we will try all means."

"We *must* try all means," replied Jeanie; "but writing winna do it—a letter canna look, and pray, and beg, and beseech, as the human voice can do to the human heart. A letter's like the music that the ladies have for their spirits—naething but black scores, compared to the same tune played or sung. It's word of mouth maun do it, or naething, Reuben."

"You are right," said Reuben, re-collecting his firmness, "and I will hope that Heaven has suggested to your kind heart and firm courage the only possible means of saving the life of this unfortunate girl. But, Jeanie, you must not take this most perilous journey alone; I have an interest in you, and I will not agree that my Jeanie throws herself away. You must even, in the present circumstances, give me a husband's right to protect you, and I will go with you myself on this journey, and assist you to do your duty by your family."

"Alas, Reuben!" said Jeanie in her turn, "this must not be; a pardon will not gie my sister her fair fame again, or make me a bride fitting for an honest man and a usefu' minister. Wha wad mind what he said in the pu'pit, that had to wife the sister of a woman that was condemned for sic wickedness!"

"But, Jeanie," pleaded her lover, "I do not believe, and I cannot believe, that Effie has done this deed."

"Heaven bless you for saying sae, Reuben!" answered Jeanie; "but she maun bear the blame o't, after all."

"But that blame, were it even justly laid on her, does not fall on you."

"Ah, Reuben, Reuben," replied the young woman, "ye ken it is a blot that spreads to kith and kin. Ichabod—as my poor father says—the glory is departed from our house: for the poorest man's house has a glory, where there are true hands, a divine heart, and an honest fame—and the last has gane frae us a'."

"But, Jeanie, consider your word and plighted faith to me; and would ye undertake such a journey without a man to protect you?—and who should that protector be but your husband?"

"You are kind and good, Reuben, and wad tak me wi' a' my shame, I doubtna. But ye canna but own that this is no time to marry or be given in marriage. Na, if that suld ever be, it maun be in another and a better season.—And, dear Reuben, ye speak of protecting me on my journey—Alas! who will protect and take care of you?—your very limbs tremble with standing for ten minutes on the floor; how could you undertake a journey as far as Lunnon?

"But I am strong—I am well," continued Butler, sinking in his seat totally exhausted, "at least I shall be quite well to-morrow."

"Ye see, and ye ken, ye maun just let me depart," said Jeanie, after a pause; and then taking his extended hand, and gazing kindly in his face, she added, "It's e'en a grief the mair to me to see you in this way. But ye maun keep up your heart for Jeanie's sake, for if she isna your wife, she will never be the wife of living man. And now gie me the paper for Mac-Callummore, and bid God speed me on my way."

There was something of romance in Jeanie's venturous resolution ; yet, on consideration, as it seemed impossible to alter it by persuasion, or to give her assistance but by advice, Butler, after some further debate, put into her hands the paper she desired, which, with the muster-roll in which it was folded up, were the sole memorials of the stout and enthusiastic Bible Butler, his grandfather. While Butler sought this document, Jeanie had time to take up his pocket Bible. " I have marked a scripture," she said, as she again laid it down, " with your kylevine pen, that will be useful to us baith. And ye maun tak the trouble, Reuben, to write a' this to my father, for, God help me, I have neither head nor hand for lang letters at ony time, forby now ; and I trust him entirely to you, and I trust you will soon be permitted to see him. And, Reuben, when ye do win to the speech o' him, mind a' the auld man's bits o' ways, for Jeanie's sake ; and dinna speak o' Latin or English terms to him, for he's o' the auld warld, and downa bide to be fashed wi' them, though I daresay he may be wrang. And dinna ye say muckle to him, but set him on speaking himsell, for he'll bring himsell mair comfort that way. And oh, Reuben, the poor lassie in yon dungeon !—But I needna bid your kind heart—gie her what comfort ye can as soon as they will let ye see her—tell her—But I maunna speak mair about her, for I maunna take leave o' ye wi' the tear in my ee, for that wadna be canny.—God bless ye, Reuben !"

To avoid so ill an omen she left the room hastily, while her features yet retained the mournful and affectionate smile which she had compelled them to wear, in order to support Butler's spirits.

It seemed as if the power of sight, of speech, and of reflection, had left him as she disappeared from the room, which she had entered and retired from so like an apparition.

EFFIE DEANS.

EFFIE DEANS, under the tender and affectionate care of her sister, had now shot up into a beautiful and blooming girl. Her Grecian-shaped head was profusely rich in waving ringlets of brown hair, which, confined by a blue snood of silk, and shading a laughing Hebe countenance, seemed the picture of health, pleasure, and contentment. Her brown russet short-gown set off a shape, which time, perhaps, might be expected to render too robust, the frequent objection to Scottish beauty, but which, in her present early age, was slender and taper, with that graceful and easy sweep of outline which at once indicates health and beautiful proportion of parts.

These growing charms, in all their juvenile profusion, had no power to shake the steadfast mind, or divert the fixed gaze, of the constant Laird of Dumbiedikes. But there was scarce another eye that could behold this living picture of health and beauty, without pausing on it with pleasure. The traveller stopped his weary horse on the eve of entering the city which was the end of his journey, to gaze at the sylph-like form that

tripped by him, with her milk-pail poised on her head, bearing
herself so erect, and stepping so light and free under her burden, that it seemed rather an ornament than an encumbrance.
The lads of the neighboring suburb, who held their evening
rendezvous for putting the stone, casting the hammer, playing
at long bowls, and other athletic exercises, watched the motions
of Effie Deans, and contended with each other which should
have the good fortune to attract her attention. Even the rigid
presbyterians of her father's persuasion, who held each indulgence of the eye and sense to be a snare at least, if not a crime,
were surprised into a moment's delight while gazing on a creature so exquisite,—instantly checked by a sigh, reproaching at
once their own weakness, and mourning that a creature so fair
should share in the common and hereditary guilt and imperfec-
tion of our nature. She was currently entitled the Lily of St.
Leonard's, a name which she deserved as much by her guileless
purity of thought, speech, and action, as by her uncommon loveliness of face and person.

Yet there were points in Effie's character, which gave rise
not only to strange doubt and anxiety on the part of Douce
David Deans, whose ideas were rigid, as may easily be supposed,
upon the subject of youthful amusements, but even of serious
apprehension to her more indulgent sister. The children of the
Scotch of the inferior classes are usually spoiled by the early indulgence of their parents; how, wherefore, and to what degree,
the lively and instructive narrative of the amiable and accomplished authoress of " Glenburnie " has saved me and all future
scribblers the trouble of recording. Effie had had a double share
of this inconsiderate and misjudged kindness. Even the strict-
ness of her father's principles could not condemn the sports of
infancy and childhood; and to the good old man, his younger

daughter, the child of his old age, seemed a child for some years after she attained the years of womanhood, was still called the "bit lassie" and "little Effie," and was permitted to run up and down uncontrolled, unless upon the Sabbath, or at the times of family worship. Her sister, with all the love and care of a mother, could not be supposed to possess the same authoritative influence; and that which she had hitherto exercised became gradually limited and diminished as Effie's advancing years entitled her, in her own conceit at least, to the right of independence and free agency. With all the innocence and goodness of disposition, therefore, which we have described, the Lily of St. Leonard's possessed a little fund of self-conceit and obstinacy, and some warmth and irritability of temper, partly natural perhaps, but certainly much increased by the unrestrained freedom of her childhood. Her character will be best illustrated by a cottage evening scene.

The careful father was absent in his well-stocked byre, foddering those useful and patient animals on whose produce his living depended, and the summer evening was beginning to close in, when Jeanie Deans began to be very anxious for the appearance of her sister, and to fear that she would not reach home before her father returned from the labor of the evening, when it was his custom to have "family exercise," and when she knew that Effie's absence would give him the most serious displeasure. These apprehensions hung heavier upon her mind, because, for several preceding evenings, Effie had disappeared about the same time, and her stay, at first so brief as scarce to be noticed, had been gradually protracted to half an hour, and an hour, and on the present occasion had considerably exceeded even this last limit. And now, Jeanie stood at the door, with her hand before her eyes to avoid the rays of the level sun, and

12

looked alternately along the various tracks which led towards their dwelling, to see if she could descry the nymph-like form of her sister. There was a wall and a stile which separated the royal domain, or King's Park, as it is called, from the public road; to this pass she frequently directed her attention, when she saw two persons appear there somewhat suddenly, as if they had walked close by the side of the wall to screen themselves from observation. One of them, a man, drew back hastily; the other, a female, crossed the stile, and advanced towards her.— It was Effie. She met her sister with that affected liveliness of manner, which, in her rank, and sometimes in those above it, females occasionally assume to hide surprise or confusion; and she carolled as she came—

> " The elfin knight sate on the brae,
>> The broom grows bonny, the broom grows fair ;
> And by there came lilting a lady so gay,
>> And we daurna gang down to the broom nae mair."

" Whisht, Effie," said her sister ; " our father's coming out o' the byre."—The damsel stinted in her song.—" Whare hae ye been sae late at e'en ? "

" It's no late, lass," answered Effie.

" It's chappit eight on every clock o' the town, and the sun's gaun down ahint the Corstorphine hills—Whare can ye hae been sae late ? "

" Nae gate," answered Effie.

" And wha was that parted wi' you at the stile ? "

" Naebody," replied Effie, once more.

" Nae gate ?—Naebody ?—I wish it may be a right gate, and a right body, that keeps folk out sae late at e'en, Effie."

"What needs ye be aye speering then at folk?" retorted Effie. "I'm sure, if ye'll ask nae questions, I'll tell ye nae lees. I never ask what brings the Laird of Dumbie-dikes glowering here like a wull-cat, (only his een's greener, and no sae gleg,) day after day, till we are a' like to gaunt our chafts aff."

"Because ye ken very weel he comes to see our father," said Jeanie, in answer to this pert remark.

"And Dominie Butler—Does he come to see our father, that's sae taen wi' his Latin words?" said Effie, delighted to find that, by carrying the war into the enemy's country, she could divert the threatened attack upon herself, and with the petulance of youth she pursued her triumph over her prudent elder sister. She looked at her with a sly air, in which there was something like irony, as she chanted, in a low but marked tone, a scrap of an old Scotch song—

> "Through the kirkyard
> I met wi' the Laird,
> The silly puir body he said me nae harm;
> But just ere 'twas dark,
> I met wi' the clerk"——

Here the songstress stopped, looked full at her sister, and, observing the tear gather in her eyes, she suddenly flung her arms round her neck, and kissed them away. Jeanie, though hurt and displeased, was unable to resist the caresses of this untaught child of nature, whose good and evil seemed to flow rather from impulse than from reflection. But as she returned the sisterly kiss, in token of perfect re-conciliation, she could not suppress the gentle reproof—

"Effie, if ye will learn fule sangs, ye might make a kinder use of them."

"And so I might, Jeanie," continued the girl, clinging to her sister's neck; " and I wish I had never learned ane o' them—and I wish we had never come here—and I wish my tongue had been blistered or I had vexed ye."

MADGE WILDFIRE.

"But these are sad tales to tell—I maun just sing a bit to keep up my heart—It's a sang that Gentle George made on me lang syne, when I went with him to Lockington wake, to see him act upon a stage, in fine clothes, with the player folk. He might have dune waur than married me that night as he promised—better wed over the mixen as over the moor, as they say in Yorkshire—he may gang further and fare waur—but that's a' ane to the sang———

    ' I'm Madge of the country, I'm Madge of the town,
    And I'm Madge of the lad I am blithest to own—
    The Lady of Beever in diamonds may shine,
    But has not a heart half so lightsome as mine.

    I am Queen of the Wake, and I'm Lady of May,
    And I lead the blithe ring round the May-pole to-day:
    The wild-fire that flashes so fair and so free,
    Was never so bright, or so bonny, as me.'

"I like that the best o' a' my sangs," continued the maniac, "because *he* made it. I am often singing it, and that's maybe the reason folk ca' me Madge Wildfire.   I aye answer to the name, though it's no my ain, for what's the use of making a fash ? "

"But ye shouldna sing upon the Sabbath, at least," said Jeanie, who, amid all her distress and anxiety, could not help being scandalized at the deportment of her companion, especially as they now approached near to the little village.

"Ay! is this Sunday ? " said Madge.   " My mother leads sic a life, wi' turning night into day, that ane loses a' count o' the days o' the week, and disna ken Sunday frae Saturday.   Besides, it's a' your whiggery—in England, folk sing when they like—And then, ye ken, you are Christiana, and I am Mercy—and ye ken, as they went on their way, they sang."   And she immediately raised one of John Bunyan's ditties :

> " ' He that is down need fear no fall,
>   He that is low no pride ;
>   He that is humble ever shall
>   Have God to be his guide.

> " ' Fulness to such a burthen is
>   That go on pilgrimage ;
>   Here little, and hereafter bliss,
>   Is best from age to age.'

"And do ye ken, Jeanie, I think there's much truth in that book, the Pilgrim's Progress.   The boy that sings that song was feeding his Father's sheep, in the Valley of Humiliation, and Mr. Great-Heart says that he lived a merrier life, and had more of the herb called heart's ease in his bosom, than they that wear silk and velvet like me, and are as bonny as I am."

They were now close by the village, one of those beautiful scenes which are so often found in merry England, where the

cottages, instead of being built in two direct lines on each side
of a dusty high-road, stand in detached groups, interspersed not
only with large oaks and elms, but with fruit-trees, so many of
which were at this time in flourish, that the grove seemed enam-
elled with their crimson and white blossoms. In the centre of
the hamlet stood the parish church and its little Gothic tower,
from which at present was heard the Sunday chime of bells.

"We will wait here until the folk are a' in the church—they
ca' the kirk a church in England, Jeanie; be sure you mind
that—for if I was gaun forward amang them, a' the gaitts o'
boys and lasses wad be crying at Madge Wildfire's tail, the little
hell-rakers! and the beadle would be as hard upon us as if it
was our fault. I like their skirling as ill as he does, I can tell
him; I'm sure I often wish there was a het peat down their
throats when they set them up that gate."

Conscious of the disorderly appearance of her own dress after
the adventure of the preceding night, and of the grotesque habit
and demeanor of her guide, and sensible how important it was
to secure an attentive and patient audience to her strange story
from some one who might have the means to protect her, Jeanie
readily acquiesced in Madge's proposal to rest under the trees,
by which they were still somewhat screened, until the commencement of service should give them an opportunity of entering the
hamlet without attracting a crowd around them. She made the
less opposition, that Madge had intimated that this was not the
village where her mother was in custody, and that the two
squires of the pad were absent in a different direction.

She sat herself down, therefore, at the foot of an oak, and
by the assistance of a placid fountain which had been dammed
up for the use of the villagers, and which served her as a natural
mirror, she began—no uncommon thing with a Scottish maiden

of her rank—to arrange her toilette in the open air, and bring
her dress, soiled and disordered as it was, into such order as the
place and circumstances admitted.

She soon perceived reason, however, to regret that she had
set about this task, however decent and necessary, in the present
time and society. Madge Wildfire, who, among other indications of insanity, had a most overweening opinion of those
charms, to which, in fact, she owed her misery, and whose mind,
like a raft upon a lake, was agitated and driven about at random
by each fresh impulse, no sooner beheld Jeanie begin to arrange
her hair, place her bonnet in order, rub the dust from her shoes
and clothes, adjust her neck-handkerchief and mittens, and so
forth, than with imitative zeal she began to bedizen and trick
herself out with shreds and remnants of beggarly finery which
she took out of a little bundle, and which, when disposed around
her person, made her appearance ten times more fantastic and
apish than it had been before.

Jeanie groaned in spirit, but dared not interfere in a matter
so delicate. Across the man's cap or riding hat which she wore,
Madge placed a broken and soiled white feather, intersected
with one which had been shed from the train of a peacock. To
her dress, which was a kind of riding-habit, she stitched, pinned,
and otherwise secured, a large furbelow of artificial flowers, all
crushed, wrinkled, and dirty, which had first bedecked a lady of
quality, then descended to her Abigail, and dazzled the inmates
of the servants'-hall. A tawdry scarf of yellow silk, trimmed
with tinsel and spangles, which had seen as hard service, and
boasted as honorable a transmission, was next flung over one
shoulder, and fell across her person in the manner of a shoulder-
belt, or baldrick. Madge then stripped off the coarse ordinary
shoes which she wore and replaced them by a pair of dirty

satin ones, spangled and embroidered to match the scarf, and
furnished with very high heels. She had cut a willow switch
in her morning's walk, almost as long as a boy's fishing-rod.
This she set herself seriously to peel, and when it was trans-
formed into such a wand as the Treasurer or High Steward
bears on public occasions, she told Jeanie that she thought they
now looked decent, as young women should do upon the Sunday morning, and that as the bells had done ringing, she was
willing to conduct her to the Interpreter's house.

Jeanie sighed heavily, to think it should be her lot on the
Lord's-day, and during kirk-time too, to parade the street of an
inhabited village with so very grotesque a comrade ; but necessity had no law, since, without a positive quarrel with the
mad woman, which, in the circumstances, would have been very
unadvisable, she could see no means of shaking herself free of
her society.

As for poor Madge, she was completely elated with personal
vanity, and the most perfect satisfaction concerning her own
dazzling dress, and superior appearance. They entered the
hamlet without being observed, except by one old woman, who,
being nearly "high-gravel blind," was only conscious that something very fine and glittering was passing by, and dropped as
deep a reverence to Madge as she would have done to a Countess.
This filled up the measure of Madge's self-approbation. She
minced, she ambled, she smiled, she simpered, and waved Jeanie
Deans forward with the condescension of a noble *chaperone*, who
has undertaken the charge of a country miss on her first journey
to the capital.

When at length they approached the church, and Jeanie
saw Madge about to enter, she would have resisted—but the
maniac took hold of her, and conceiving that she might receive

13

bodily hurt before she could obtain the assistance of any one, she thought it wise to follow quietly. No sooner had Madge put her foot upon the pavement, and become sensible that she was the object of attention to the spectators, than she resumed all her fantastic extravagance of deportment. She swam rather than walked up the centre isle, dragging Jeanie after her. Madge's airs were at length fortunately cut short by her encountering the look of the clergyman. She hastily opened a pew near her, and entered, dragging Jeanie in. Kicking Jeanie on the shins, by way of hint that she should follow her example, she sunk her head upon her hand.

LUCY ASHTON.

Lucy Ashton's exquisitely beautiful, yet somewhat girlish features, were formed to express peace of mind, serenity, and indifference to the tinsel of worldly pleasure. Her locks, which were of shadowy gold, divided on a brow of exquisite whiteness, like a gleam of broken and pallid sunshine upon a hill of snow. The expression of the countenance was in the last degree gentle, soft, timid, and feminine, and seemed rather to shrink from the most casual look of a stranger, than to court his admiration. Something there was of a Madonna cast, perhaps the result of delicate health, and of residence in a family where the dispositions of the inmates were fiercer, more active, and energetic, than her own.

Yet her passiveness of disposition was by no means owing to an indifferent or unfeeling mind. Left to the impulse of her own taste and feelings, Lucy Ashton was peculiarly accessible to those of a romantic cast. Her secret delight was in the old legendary tales of ardent devotion and unalterable affection, chequered as they so often are with strange adventures and supernatural horrors. This was her favored fairy realm, and here she erected her aerial palaces. But it was only in secret that she labored at this delusive, though delightful architecture. In her retired chamber, or in the woodland bower which she had chosen for her own, and called after her name, she was in fancy distributing the prizes at the tournament, or raining down influence from her eyes on the valiant combatants; or she was wandering in the wilderness with Una, under escort of the generous lion; or she was identifying herself with the simple, yet noble-minded Miranda, in the isle of wonder and enchantment.

She sat upon one of the disjointed stones of the ancient fountain, and seemed to watch the progress of its current, as it bubbled forth to daylight, in gay and sparkling profusion, from under the shadow of the ribbed and darksome vault, with which veneration, or perhaps remorse, had canopied its source. To a superstitious eye, Lucy Ashton, folded in her plaided mantle, with her long hair partly escaping from the snood and falling upon her silver neck, might have suggested the idea of the murdered Nymph of the Fountain. But Ravenswood only saw a female exquisitely beautiful, and rendered yet more so in his eyes—how could it be otherwise—by the consciousness that she had placed her affections on him. As he gazed on her, he felt his fixed resolution melting like wax in the sun, and hastened, therefore, from his concealment in the neighboring thicket. She saluted him, but did not arise from the stone on which she was seated.

"My mad-cap brother," she said, "has left me, but I expect him back in a few minutes—for fortunately, as any thing pleases him for a moment, nothing has charms for him much longer."

Ravenswood did not feel the power of informing Lucy that her brother meditated a distant excursion, and would not return in haste. He sat himself down on the grass, at some little distance from Miss Ashton, and both were silent for a short space.

"I like this spot," said Lucy at length, as if she had found the silence embarrassing; "the bubbling murmur of the clear fountain, the waving of the trees, the profusion of grass and wild-flowers, that rise among the ruins, make it like a scene in romance. I think, too, I have heard it is a spot connected with the legendary lore which I love so well."

"It has been thought," answered Ravenswood, "a fatal spot to my family; and I have some reason to term it so, for it was here I first saw Miss Ashton—and it is here I must take my leave of her for ever."

The blood, which the first part of this speech called into Lucy's cheeks, was speedily expelled by its conclusion.

"To take leave of us, Master?" she exclaimed; "what can have happened to hurry you away?—I know Alice hates—I mean dislikes my father—and I hardly understood her humor to-day, it was so mysterious. But I am certain my father is sincerely grateful for the high service you rendered us. Let me hope, that having won your friendship hardly, we shall not lose it lightly."

"Lose it, Miss Ashton?" said the Master of Ravenswood. "No—wherever my fortune calls me—whatever she inflicts upon me—it is your friend—your sincere friend, who acts or suffers. But there is a fate on me, and I must go, or I shall add the ruin of others to my own."

Lucy covered her face with her hands, and the tears, in spite of her, forced their way between her fingers. "Forgive me," said Ravenswood, taking her right hand, which, after slight resistance, she yielded to him, still continuing to shade her face with the left—"I am too rude—too rough—too intractable to deal with any being so soft and gentle as you are. Forget that so stern a vision has crossed your path of life—and let me pursue mine, sure that I can meet with no worse misfortune after the moment it divides me from your side."

Lucy wept on, but her tears were less bitter. Each attempt which the Master made to explain his purpose of departure, only proved a new evidence of his desire to stay; until, at length, instead of bidding her farewell, he gave his faith to her for ever, and received her troth in return. The whole passed so suddenly, and arose so much out of the immediate impulse of the moment, that ere the Master of Ravenswood could reflect upon the consequences of the step which he had taken, their lips, as well as their hands, had pledged the sincerity of their affection.

" Lucy," he said, " I have sacrificed to you projects of vengeance long nursed, and sworn to with ceremonies little better than heathen—I sacrificed them to your image, ere I knew the worth which it represented. In the evening which succeeded my poor father's funeral, I cut a lock from my hair, and, as it consumed in the fire, I swore that my rage and revenge should pursue his enemies, until they shrivelled before me like that scorched-up symbol of annihilation."

" It was a deadly sin," said Lucy, turning pale, " to make a vow so fatal."

" I acknowledge it," said Ravenswood, " and it had been a worse crime to keep it. It was for your sake that I abjured these purposes of revenge, though I scarce knew that such was the argument by which I was conquered, until I saw you once more, and became conscious of the influence you possessed over me."

" And why do you now," said Lucy, " recall sentiments so terrible—sentiments so inconsistent with those you profess for me—with those your importunity has prevailed on me to acknowledge."

LADY ROWENA.

THE bustling Prior of Jorvaulx had reminded Prince John, in a whisper, that the victor must now display his good judgment, instead of his valor, by selecting from among the beauties who graced the galleries, a lady, who should fill the throne of the Queen of Beauty and of Love, and deliver the price of the tourney upon the ensuing day. The Prince accordingly made a sign with his truncheon, as the Knight passed him in his second career around the lists. The Knight turned towards the throne, and sinking his lance, until the point was within a foot of the ground, remained motionless, as if expecting John's commands; while all admired the sudden dexterity with which he instantly reduced his fiery steed from a state of violent emotion and high excitation to the stillness of an equestrian statue.

"Sir Disinherited Knight," said Prince John, "since that is the only title by which we can address you, it is now your duty, as well as privilege, to name the fair lady, who, as Queen of Honor and of Love, is to preside over next day's festival. If, as a stranger in our land, you should require the aid of other judgment to guide your own, we can only say that Alicia, the

14

daughter of our gallant knight Waldemar Fitzurse, has at our
court long been held the first in beauty as in place. Nevertheless, it is your undoubted prerogative to confer on whom you
please this crown, by the delivery of which to the lady of your
choice, the election of to-morrow's Queen will be formal and
complete. Raise your lance."

The knight obeyed; and Prince John placed upon its point
a coronet of green satin, having around its edge a circlet of gold,
the upper edge of which was relieved by arrow-points and hearts
placed interchangeably, like the strawberry leaves and balls upon
a ducal crown.

The Disinherited Knight passed the gallery close to that of
the Prince, in which the Lady Alicia was seated in the full pride
of triumphant beauty, and, pacing forwards as slowly as he had
hitherto rode swiftly around the lists, he seemed to exercise his
right of examining the numerous fair faces which adorned that
splendid circle.

It was worth while to see the different conduct of the beauties who underwent this examination, during the time it was
proceeding. Some blushed, some assumed an air of pride and
dignity, some looked straight forward, and essayed to seem utterly unconscious of what was going on, some drew back in
alarm, which was perhaps affected, some endeavored to forbear
smiling, and there were two or three who laughed outright.
There were also some who dropped their veils over their charms;
but as the Wardour Manuscript says these were fair ones of ten
years standing, it may be supposed that, having had their full
share of such vanities, they were willing to withdraw their
claim in order to give a fair chance to the rising beauties of the
age.

At length the champion paused beneath the balcony in which

the Lady Rowena was placed, and the expectation of the spectators was excited to the utmost.

Formed in the best proportions of her sex, Rowena was tall
in stature, yet not so much so as to attract observation on account of superior height. Her complexion was exquisitely fair,
but the noble cast of her head and features prevented the in-
sipidity which sometimes attaches to fair beauties. Her clear
blue eye, which sat enshrined beneath a graceful eyebrow of
brown, sufficiently marked to give expression to the forehead,
seemed capable to kindle as well as melt, to command as well as
to beseech. If mildness were the more natural expression of
such a combination of features, it was plain, that in the present
instance, the exercise of habitual superiority, and the reception
of general homage, had given to the Saxon lady a loftier character, which mingled with and qualified that bestowed by nature.
Her profuse hair, of a color betwixt brown and flaxen, was arranged in a fanciful and graceful manner in numerous ringlets,
to form which, art had probably aided nature. These locks
were braided with gems, and being worn at full length, intimated the noble birth and free-born condition of the maiden. A
golden chain, to which was attached a small reliquary of the
same metal, hung round her neck. She wore bracelets on her
arms, which were bare. Her dress was an under-gown and kirtle of pale sea-green silk, over which hung a long loose robe,
which reached to the ground, having very wide sleeves, which
came down, however, very little below the elbow. This robe
was crimson, and manufactured out of the very finest wool. A
veil of silk, interwoven with gold, was attached to the upper
part of it, which could be, at the wearer's pleasure, either drawn
over the face and bosom, after the Spanish fashion, or disposed
as a sort of drapery round the shoulders.

Whether from indecision or some other motive of hesitation, the champion of the day remained stationary for more than a minute, while the eyes of the silent audience were riveted upon his motions; and then, gradually and gracefully sinking the point of his lance, he deposited the coronet which it supported at the feet of the fair Rowena. The trumpets instantly sounded, while the heralds proclaimed the Lady Rowena the Queen of Beauty and of Love for the ensuing day, menacing with suitable penalties those who should be disobedient to her authority. They then repeated their cry of Largesse, to which Cedric, in the height of his joy, replied by an ample donative, and to which Athelstane, though less promptly, added one equally large.

There was some murmuring among the damsels of Norman descent, who were as much unused to see the preference given to a Saxon beauty, as the Norman nobles were to sustain defeat in the games of chivalry which they themselves had introduced. But these sounds of disaffection were drowned by the popular shout of "Long live the Lady Rowena, the chosen and lawful Queen of Love and Beauty!" To which many in the lower area added, "Long live the Saxon Princess! long live the race of the immortal Alfred!"

However unacceptable these sounds might be to Prince John, and to those around him, he saw himself nevertheless obliged to confirm the nomination of the victor, and accordingly calling to horse, he left his throne, and mounting his jennet, accompanied by his train, he again entered the lists. The Prince paused a moment beneath the gallery of the Lady Alicia, to whom he paid his compliments, observing at the same time, to those around him—" By my halidome, sirs! if the Knight's feats in arms have shown that he hath limbs and sinews, his choice hath no less proved that his eyes are none of the clearest."

It was on this occasion, as during his whole life, John's misfortune, not perfectly to understand the characters of those whom he wished to conciliate. Waldemar Fitzurse was rather offended than pleased at the Prince stating thus broadly an opinion, that his daughter had been slighted.

"I know no right of chivalry," he said, " more precious or inalienable than that of each free knight to choose his lady-love by his own judgment. My daughter courts distinction from no one; and in her own character, and in her own sphere, will never fail to receive the full proportion of that which is her due."

Prince John replied not; but, spurring his horse, as if to give vent to his vexation, he made the animal bound forward to the gallery where Rowena was seated, with the crown still at her feet.

"Assume," he said, " fair lady, the mark of your sovereignty, to which none vows homage more sincerely than ourself, John of Anjou ; and if it please you to-day, with your noble sire and friends, to grace our banquet in the Castle of Ashby, we shall learn to know the empress to whose service we devote to-morrow."

Rowena remained silent, and Cedric answered for her in his native Saxon.

"The Lady Rowena," he said, "possesses not the language in which to reply to your courtesy, or to sustain her part in your festival. I also, and the noble Athelstane of Coningsburgh, speak only the language and practise only the manners of our fathers. We therefore decline with thanks your Highness's courteous invitation to the banquet. To-morrow the Lady Rowena will take upon her the state to which she has been called by the free election of the victor Knight, confirmed by the acclamations of the people."

So saying, he lifted the coronet, and placed it upon Rowena's head, in token of her acceptance of the temporary authority assigned to her.

REBECCA.

THE figure of Rebecca might have compared with the proud-
est beauties of England. Her form was exquisitely symmetri-
cal, and was shown to advantage by a sort of Eastern dress,
which was worn according to the fashion of the females of her
nation. Her turban of yellow silk suited well with the darkness of her complexion. The brilliancy of her eyes, the superb
arch of her eyebrows, her well-formed aquiline nose, her teeth
as white as pearl, and the profusion of her sable tresses, which,
each arranged in its own little spiral of twisted curls, fell down
upon as much of a lovely neck and bosom as a simarre of the
richest Persian silk, exhibiting flowers in their natural colors
embossed upon a purple ground, permitted to be visible—all
these constituted a combination of loveliness, which yielded not
to the most beautiful of the maidens who surrounded her. It
is true, that of the golden and pearl-studded clasps, which closed
her vest from the throat to the waist, the three uppermost were
left unfastened on account of the heat, which something enlarged
the prospect to which we allude. A diamond necklace, with
pendants of inestimable value, were by this means also made
more conspicuous. The feather of an ostrich, fastened in her

turban by an agraffe set with brilliants, was another distinction
of the beautiful Jewess, scoffed and sneered at by proud dames,
but secretly envied by those who affected to deride them.

This beauty was now to expect a fate even more dreadful
than that of Rowena; for what probability was there that
either softness or ceremony would be used towards one of her
oppressed race, whatever shadow of these might be preserved towards a Saxon heiress? Yet had the Jewess this advantage,
that she was better prepared by habits of thought, and by
natural strength of mind, to encounter the dangers to which she
was exposed. Of a strong and observing character, even from
her earliest years, the pomp and wealth which her father displayed within his walls, or which she witnessed in the houses of
other wealthy Hebrews, had not been able to blind her to the
precarious circumstances under which they were enjoyed. Like
Damocles at his celebrated banquet, Rebecca perpetually beheld,
amid that gorgeous display, the sword which was suspended
over the heads of her people by a single hair. These reflections
had tamed and brought down to a pitch of sounder judgment
a temper, which, under other circumstances, might have waxed
haughty, supercilious, and obstinate.

Her first care was to inspect the apartment; but it afforded
few hopes either of escape or protection. It contained neither
secret passage nor trap-door, and unless where the door by
which she had entered joined the main building, seemed to be
circumscribed by the round exterior wall of the turret. The
door had no inside bolt or bar. The single window opened
upon an embattled space surmounting the turret, which gave
Rebecca, at first sight, some hopes of escaping; but she soon
found it had no communication with any other part of the bat-
tlements, being an isolated bartisan, or balcony, secured, as

usual, by a parapet, with embrasures, at which a few archers might be stationed for defending the turret, and flanking with their shot the wall of the castle on that side.

The prisoner trembled, however, and changed color, when a step was heard on the stair, and the door of the turret-chamber slowly opened, and a tall man, dressed as one of those banditti to whom they owed their misfortune, slowly entered, and shut the door behind him; his cap, pulled down upon his brows, concealed the upper part of his face, and he held his mantle in such a manner as to muffle the rest. In this guise, as if prepared for the execution of some deed, at the thought of which he was himself ashamed, he stood before the affrighted prisoner; yet, ruffian as his dress bespoke him, he seemed at a loss to express what purpose had brought him thither, so that Rebecca, making an effort upon herself, had time to anticipate his explanation. She had already unclasped two costly bracelets and a collar, which she hastened to proffer to the supposed outlaw, concluding naturally that to gratify his avarice was to bespeak his favor.

"Take these," she said, "good friend, and for God's sake be merciful to me and my aged father! These ornaments are of value, yet are they trifling to what he would bestow to obtain our dismissal from this castle, free and uninjured."

"Fair flower of Palestine," replied the outlaw, "these pearls are orient, but they yield in whiteness to your teeth; the diamonds are brilliant, but they cannot match your eyes; and ever since I have taken up this wild trade, I have made a vow to prefer beauty to wealth."

"Do not do yourself such wrong," said Rebecca; "take ransom, and have mercy!—Gold will purchase you pleasure,—to misuse us, could only bring thee remorse.

15

"It is well spoken," replied the outlaw in French, finding
it difficult probably to sustain, in Saxon, a conversation which Rebecca had opened in that language ; " but know, bright lily of the
vale of Baca ! that thy father is already in the hands of a powerful
alchemist, who knows how to convert into gold and silver even
the rusty bars of a dungeon grate. Thy ransom must be paid
by love and beauty, and in no other coin will I accept it."

"Thou art no outlaw," said Rebecca, in the same language
in which he addressed her ; " no outlaw had refused such offers.
No outlaw in this land uses the dialect in which thou hast spok-
en.   Thou art no outlaw, but a Norman—a Norman, noble
perhaps in birth—Oh, be so in thy actions, and cast off this
fearful mask of outrage and violence ! "

The eyes of the Templar flashed fire—" Hearken," he said,
"Rebecca ; I have hitherto spoken mildly to thee, but now my
language shall be that of a conqueror. Thou art the captive of
my bow and spear—subject to my will by the laws of all nations ; nor will I abate an inch of my right, or abstain from
taking by violence what thou refusest to entreaty or necessity."

"Stand back," said Rebecca—" stand back, and hear me
ere thou offerest to commit a sin so deadly ! My strength thou
mayest indeed overpower, for God made woman weak, and
trusted their defence to man's generosity. But I will proclaim
thy villany, Templar, from one end of Europe to the other. I
will owe to the superstition of thy brethren what their compassion might refuse me. Each Preceptory—each Chapter of thy
Order, shall learn, that, like a heretic, thou hast sinned with a
Jewess. Those who tremble not at thy crime, will hold thee ac-
cursed for having so far dishonored the cross thou wearest, as
to follow a daughter of my people."

"Thou art keen-witted, Jewess," replied the Templar, well

aware of the truth of what she spoke, and that by the rules of his Order, upon such intrigues as he now prosecuted degradation followed; "but loud must be thy voice of complaint, if it is heard beyond the iron walls of this castle. Submit to thy fate—embrace our religion, and thou shalt go forth in such state, that many a Norman lady shall yield as well in pomp as in beauty to the favorite of the best lance among the defenders of the Temple."

"Submit to my fate!" said Rebecca—" and, sacred Heaven! to what fate?—embrace thy religion! and what religion can it be that harbors such a villain?—*thou* the best lance of the Templars!—Craven knight!—forsworn priest! I spit at thee, and I defy thee.—The God of Abraham's promise hath opened an escape to his daughter—even from this abyss of infamy!"

As she spoke, she threw open the lattice window which led to the bartisan, and in an instant after, stood on the very verge of the parapet, with not the slightest screen between her and the tremendous depth below. Unprepared for such a desperate effort, for she had hitherto stood perfectly motionless, Bois-Guilbert had neither time to intercept nor to stop her. As he offered to advance, she exclaimed, "Remain where thou art, proud Templar, or at thy choice advance!—one foot nearer, and I plunge myself from the precipice; my body shall be crushed out of the very form of humanity upon the stones of that court-yard, ere it become the victim of thy brutality!"

The Templar hesitated, and a resolution which had never yielded to pity or distress, gave way to his admiration of her fortitude. "Come down," he said, "rash girl! I swear by earth, and sea, and sky, I will offer thee no offence."

"I will not trust thee, Templar," said Rebecca.

"May my arms be reversed, and my name dishonored," said

Brian de Bois-Guilbert, "if thou shalt have reason to complain of me! Many a law, many a commandment have I broken, but my word, never."

"I will then trust thee," said Rebecca, "thus far;" and she descended from the verge of the battlement, but remained standing close by one of the embrasures, or *machicolles*, as they were then called. "Here," she said, "I take my stand. Remain where thou art, and if thou shalt attempt to diminish by one step the distance now between us, thou shalt see that the Jewish maiden will rather trust her soul with God, than her honor to the Templar!"

While Rebecca spoke thus, her high and firm resolve, which corresponded so well with the expressive beauty of her countenance, gave to her looks, air, and manner, a dignity that seemed more than mortal. Her glance quailed not, her cheek blanched not, for the fear of a fate so instant and so horrible; on the contrary, the thought that she had her fate at her command, and could escape at will from infamy to death, gave a yet deeper color of carnation to her complexion, and a yet more brilliant fire to her eye. Bois-Guilbert, proud himself and high-spirited, thought he had never beheld beauty so animated and so commanding.

"Let there be peace between us, Rebecca," he said.

"Peace, if thou wilt," answered Rebecca—"peace—but with this space between."

"Thou needst no longer fear me," said Bois-Guilbert.

"I fear thee not," replied she; "thanks to him that reared this dizzy tower so high, that naught could fall from it and live —thanks to him, and to the God of Israel!—I fear thee not!"

THE WHITE LADY OF AVENEL.

HALBERT, his head unbonneted, his features swelled with jealous anger, and the tear still in his eye, sped up the wild and upper extremity of the little valley of Glendearg with the speed of a roebuck, choosing, as if in desperate defiance of the difficulties of the way, the wildest and most dangerous paths, and voluntarily exposing himself a hundred times to dangers which he might have escaped by turning a little aside from them. It seemed as if he wished his course to be as straight as that of the arrow to its mark.

He arrived at length in a narrow and secluded *cleuch*, or deep ravine, which ran down into the valley, and contributed a scanty rivulet to the supply of the brook with which Glendearg is watered. Up this he sped with the same precipitate haste which had marked his departure from the tower ; nor did he pause and look round until he had reached the fountain from which the rivulet had its rise.

Here Halbert stopped short, and cast a gloomy and almost a frightened glance around him. A huge rock rose in front, from a cleft of which grew a wild holly tree, whose dark green branches rustled over the spring which arose beneath. The

banks on either hand rose so high, and approached each other
so closely, that it was only when the sun was at its meridian
height, and during the summer solstice, that its rays could reach
the bottom of the chasm in which he stood. But it was now
summer, and the hour was noon, so that the unwonted reflection of the sun was dancing in the pellucid fountain.

"Already have I endured the vision," said Halbert to himself, "and why not again? What can it do to me, who am a
man of lith and limb, and have by my side my father's sword?
Does my heart beat—do my hairs bristle, at the thought of
calling up a painted shadow, and how should I face a band of
Southrons in flesh and blood? By the soul of the first Glendinning, I will make proof of the charm!"

He cast the leathern brogue or buskin from his right foot,
planted himself in a firm posture, unsheathed his sword, and
first looking around to collect his resolution, he bowed three
times deliberately towards the holly tree, and as often to the
little fountain, repeating at the same time, with a determined
voice, the following rhyme:

> "Thrice to the holly brake—
> Thrice to the well:—
> I bid thee awake,
> White maid of Avenel!

> "Noon gleams on the Lake—
> Noon glows on the Fell—
> Wake thee, O wake,
> White maid of Avenel!"

These lines were hardly uttered, when there stood the figure
of a female clothed in white, within three steps of Halbert Glendinning.

"I guess, 'twas frightful there to see
A lady richly clad as she—
Beautiful exceedingly."

"There's something in that ancient superstition,
Which, erring as it is, our fancy loves.
The spring that, with its thousand crystal bubbles,
Bursts from the bosom of some desert rock
In secret solitude, may well be deem'd
The haunt of something purer, more refined,
And mightier than ourselves."

His terror for the moment overcame his natural courage, as well as the strong resolution which he had formed, that the figure which he had now twice seen should not a third time daunt him. But it would seem there is something thrilling and abhorrent to flesh and blood, in the consciousness that we stand in presence of a being in form like to ourselves, but so different in faculties and nature, that we can neither understand its purposes nor calculate its means of pursuing them.

Halbert stood silent, and gasped for breath, his hairs erecting themselves on his head—his mouth open—his eyes fixed, and, as the sole remaining sign of his late determined purpose, his sword pointed towards the apparition. At length, with a voice of ineffable sweetness, the White Lady, for by that name we shall distinguish this being, sung, or rather chanted, the following lines:

"Youth of the dark eye, wherefore didst thou call me?
Wherefore art thou here, if terrors can appall thee?
He that seeks to deal with us must know nor fear nor failing!
To coward and churl our speech is dark, our gifts are unavailing.
The breeze that brought me hither now must sweep Egyptian ground,
The fleecy cloud on which I ride for Araby is bound;

The fleecy cloud is drifting by, the breeze sighs for my stay,
For I must sail a thousand miles before the close of day."

The astonishment of Halbert began once more to give way
to his resolution, and he gained voice enough to say, though
with a faltering accent, " In the name of God, what art thou? "
The answer was in melody of a different tone and measure :

"What I am I must not show—
What I am thou couldst not know—
Something betwixt heaven and hell—
Something that neither stood nor fell—
Something that through thy wit or will
May work thee good—may work thee ill.
Neither substance quite, nor shadow,
Haunting lonely moor and meadow,
Dancing by the haunted spring,
Riding on the whirlwind's wing;
Aping in fantastic fashion
Every change of human passion,
While o'er our frozen minds they pass,
Like shadows from the mirror'd glass.
Wayward, fickle is our mood,
Hovering betwixt bad and good,
Happier than brief-dated man,
Living twenty times his span;
Far less happy, for we have
Help nor hope beyond the grave!
Man awakes to joy or sorrow;
Ours the sleep that knows no morrow.
This is all that I can show—
This is all that thou mayst know."

The White Lady paused, and appeared to await an answer;
but as Halbert hesitated how to frame his speech, the vision

seemed gradually to fade, and become more and more incorpo-
real. Justly guessing this to be a symptom of her disappear-
ance, Halbert compelled himself to say, " Lady, when I saw you
in the glen, and when you brought back the black book of Mary
of Avenel, thou didst say I should one day learn to read it."
The White Lady replied :

> " Ay! and I taught thee the word and the spell,
> To waken me here by the Fairies' Well.
> But thou hast loved the heron and hawk
> More than to seek my haunted walk ;
> And thou hast loved the lance and the sword
> More than good text and holy word;
> And thou hast loved the deer to track,
> More than the lines and the letters black ;
> And thou art a ranger of moss and of wood,
> And scornest the nurture of gentle blood."

" I will do so no longer, fair maiden," said Halbert ; " I desire to learn ; and thou didst promise me, that when I did so
desire, thou wouldst be my helper ; I am no longer afraid of thy
presence, and I am no longer regardless of instruction." As he
uttered these words, the figure of the White Maiden grew gradually as distinct as it had been at first ; and what had well-nigh
faded into an ill-defined and colorless shadow, again assumed an
appearance at least of corporeal consistency, although the hues
were less vivid, and the outline of the figure less distinct and
defined—so at least it seemed to Halbert—than those of an ordinary inhabitant of the earth. " Wilt thou grant my request,"
he said, " fair lady, and give to my keeping the holy book which
Mary of Avenel has so often wept for ? "
The White Lady replied :

16

"Thy craven fear my truth accused,
Thine idlehood my trust abused ;
He that draws to harbor late,
Must sleep without, or burst the gate.
There is a star for thee, which burn'd,
Its influence wanes, its course is turn'd ;
Valor and constancy alone
Can bring thee back the chance that's flown."

"If I have been a loiterer, Lady," answered young Glendinning, "thou shalt now find me willing to press forward with
double speed. Other thoughts have filled my mind, other
thoughts have engaged my heart, within a brief period—and by
Heaven, other occupations shall henceforward fill up my time.
I have lived in this day the space of years—I came hither a boy
—I will return a man—a man, such as may converse not only
with his own kind, but with whatever God permits to be visible
to him. I will learn the contents of that mysterious volume—I
will learn why the Lady of Avenel loved it—why the priests
feared, and would have stolen it—why thou didst twice recover
it from their hands. What mystery is wrapt in it? Speak, I
conjure thee ! " The Lady assumed an air peculiarly sad and
solemn, as, drooping her head, and folding her arms on her bosom, she replied :

"Within that awful volume lies
The mystery of mysteries !
Happiest they of human race,
To whom God has granted grace
To read, to fear, to hope, to pray,
To lift the latch, and force the way ;
And better had they ne'er been born,
Who read to doubt, or read to scorn.

"Give me the volume, Lady," said young Glendinning. "They call me idle—they call me dull—in this pursuit my industry shall not fail, nor, with God's blessing, shall my understanding. Give me the volume." The apparition again replied :

> "Many a fathom dark and deep
> I have laid the book to sleep ;
> Ethereal fires around it glowing—
> Ethereal music ever flowing—
> The sacred pledge of Heav'n
> All things revere,
> Each in his sphere,
> Save man, for whom 'twas giv'n :
> Lend thy hand, and thou shalt spy
> Things ne'er seen by mortal eye."

Halbert Glendinning boldly reached his hand to the White Lady.

"Fearest thou to go with me ?" she said, as his hand trembled at the soft and cold touch of her own—

> "Fearest thou to go with me?
> Still it is free to thee
> A peasant to dwell :
> Thou mayst drive the dull steer,
> And chase the king's deer,
> But never more come near
> This haunted well."

"If what thou sayest be true," said the undaunted boy, "my destinies are higher than thine own. There shall be neither well nor wood which I dare not visit. No fear of aught, natural or supernatural, shall bar my path through my native valley."

He had scarce uttered the words, when they both descended through the earth with a rapidity which took away Halbert's breath and every other sensation, saving that of being hurried on with the utmost velocity. At length they stopped with a shock so sudden, that the mortal journeyer through that unknown space must have been thrown down with violence, had he not been upheld by his supernatural companion.

It was more than a minute, ere, looking around him, he beheld a grotto, or natural cavern, composed of the most splendid spars and crystals, which returned in a thousand prismatic hues the light of a brilliant flame that glowed on an altar of alabaster. This altar with its fire, formed the central point of the grotto, which was of a round form, and very high in the roof, resembling in some respects the dome of a cathedral. Corresponding to the four points of the compass, there went off four long galleries, or arcades, constructed of the same brilliant materials with the dome itself, and the termination of which was lost in darkness.

No human imagination can conceive, or words suffice to describe, the glorious radiance, which, shot fiercely forth by the flame, was returned from so many hundred thousand points of reflection, afforded by the sparry pillars and their numerous angular crystals. The fire itself did not remain steady and unmoved, but rose and fell, sometimes ascending in a brilliant pyramid of condensed flame half way up the lofty expanse, and again fading into a softer and more rosy hue, and hovering, as it were, on the surface of the altar, to collect its strength for another powerful exertion. There was no visible fuel by which it was fed, nor did it emit either smoke or vapor of any kind.

What was of all the most remarkable, the black volume so

often mentioned lay not only unconsumed, but untouched in the slightest degree, amid this intensity of fire, which, while it seemed to be of force sufficient to melt adamant, had no effect whatever on the sacred book thus subjected to its utmost influence.

The White Lady, having paused long enough to let young Glendinning take a complete survey of what was around him, now said, in her usual chant,

> " Here lies the volume thou boldly hast sought ;
> Touch it and take it,—'twill dearly be bought ! "

Familiarized in some degree with marvels, and desperately desirous of showing the courage he had boasted, Halbert plunged his hand, without hesitation, into the flame, trusting to the rapidity of the motion, to snatch out the volume before the fire could greatly affect it. But he was much disappointed. The flame instantly caught upon his sleeve, and though he withdrew his hand immediately, yet his arm was so dreadfully scorched, that he had well-nigh screamed with pain. He suppressed the natural expression of anguish, however, and only intimated the agony which he felt by a contortion and a muttered groan. The White Lady passed her cold hand over his arm, and ere she had finished the following metrical chant, his pain had entirely gone, and no mark of the scorching was visible :

> " Rash thy deed,
> Mortal weed
> To immortal flames applying ;
> Rasher trust
> Has thing of dust,
> On his own weak worth relying :

> Strip thee of such fences vain,
> Strip, and prove thy luck again."

Obedient to what he understood to be the meaning of his
conductress, Halbert bared his arm to the shoulder, throwing
down the remains of his sleeve, which no sooner touched the
floor on which he stood than it collected itself together, shrivelled itself up, and was without any visible fire reduced to light
tinder, which a sudden breath of wind dispersed into empty
space. The White Lady, observing the surprise of the youth,
immediately repeated—

> "Mortal warp and mortal woof
> Cannot brook this charmed roof;
> All that mortal art hath wrought,
> In our cell returns to nought.
> The molten gold returns to clay,
> The polish'd diamond melts away;
> All is alter'd, all is flown,
> Nought stands fast but truth alone.
> Not for that thy quest give o'er :
> Courage! prove thy chance once more."

Emboldened by her words, Halbert Glendinning made a
second effort, and, plunging his bare arm into the flame, took
out the sacred volume without feeling either heat or incon-
venience of any kind. Astonished, and almost terrified, at his
own success, he beheld the flame collect itself, and shoot up
into one long and final stream, which seemed as if it would ascend to the very roof of the cavern, and then sinking as suddenly, became totally extinguished. The deepest darkness
ensued ; but Halbert had no time to consider his situation, for
the White Lady had already caught his hand, and they ascended

to upper air with the same velocity with which they had sunk into the earth.

They stood by the fountain in the Corri-nan-shian when they emerged from the bowels of the earth ; but on casting a bewildered glance around him, the youth was surprised to observe, that the shadows had fallen far to the east, and that the day was well-nigh spent. He gazed on his conductress for explanation, but her figure began to fade before his eyes—her cheeks grew paler, her features less distinct, her form became shadowy, and blended itself with the mist which was ascending the hollow ravine. What had late the symmetry of form, and the delicate, yet clear hues of feminine beauty, now resembled the flitting and pale ghost of some maiden who had died for love, as it is seen, indistinctly and by moonlight, by her perjured lover.

" Stay, spirit ! " said the youth, emboldened by his success in the subterranean dome, " thy kindness must not leave me, as one encumbered with a weapon he knows not how to wield. Thou must teach me the art to read, and to understand, this volume, else what avails it me that I possess it ? "

But the figure of the White Lady still waned before his eyes, until it became an outline as pale and indistinct as that of the moon, when the winter morning is far advanced : and ere she had ended the following chant, she was entirely invisible :—

" Alas ! alas !
　Not ours the grace
　These holy characters to trace :
　　Idle forms of painted air,
　　Not to us is given to share
　　The boon bestow'd on Adam's race :

> With patience bide,
> Heaven will provide
> The fitting time, the fitting guide."

The form was already gone, and now the voice itself had melted away in melancholy cadence, softening, as if the Being who spoke had been slowly wafted from the spot where she had commenced her melody.

CATHERINE SEYTON.

They entered a low room, in which a third female was seated. This apartment was the first Roland had observed in the mansion which was furnished with movable seats, and with a wooden table, over which was laid a piece of tapestry. A carpet was spread on the floor, there was a grate in the chimney, and, in brief, the apartment had the air of being habitable and inhabited.

But Roland's eyes found better employment than to make observations on the accommodations of the chamber; for this second female inhabitant of the mansion seemed something very different from any thing he had yet seen there. A this first entry, she had greeted with a silent and low obeisance the two aged matrons, then glancing her eyes towards Roland, she adjusted a veil which hung back over her shoulders, so as to bring it over her face ; an operation which she performed with much modesty, but without either affected haste or embarrassed timidity.

During this manœuvre, Roland had time to observe that the face was that of a girl apparently not much past sixteen, and that the eyes were at once soft and brilliant. To these very

17

favorable observations was added the certainty, that the fair object to whom they referred possessed an excellent shape, border-
ing perhaps on *embonpoint*, and therefore rather that of a Hebe
than of a Sylph, but beautifully formed, and shown to great advantage by the close jacket and petticoat which she wore after
a foreign fashion, the last not quite long enough absolutely to
conceal a very pretty foot which rested on a bar of the table at
which she sat; her round arms and taper fingers very busily
employed in repairing the piece of tapestry which was spread on
it, which exhibited several deplorable fissures, enough to demand the utmost skill of the most expert seamstress.

It is to be remarked, that it was by stolen glances that
Roland Græme contrived to ascertain these interesting particulars; and he thought he could once or twice, notwithstanding
the texture of the veil, detect the damsel in the act of taking
similar cognizance of his own person. The matrons in the
mean while continued their separate conversation, eying from
time to time the young people, in a manner which left Roland
in no doubt that they were the subject of their conversation.
At length he distinctly heard Magdalen Græme say these words
—"Nay, my sister, we must give them opportunity to speak
together, and to become acquainted; they must be personally
known to each other, or how shall they be able to execute what
they are intrusted with?"

It seemed as if the matron, not fully satisfied with her
friend's reasoning, continued to offer some objections; but they
were borne down by her more dictatorial friend.

"It must be so," she said, "my dear sister; let us therefore go forth on the balcony, to finish our conversation.—And
do you," she added, addressing Roland and the girl, "become
acquainted with each other."

With this she stepped up to the young woman, and raising her veil, discovered features which, whatever might be their ordinary complexion, were now covered with a universal blush.

"Remember, Catherine," she said, "who thou art, and for what destined."

The matron then retreated with Magdalen Græme through one of the casements of the apartment, that opened on a large broad balcony, which, with its ponderous balustrade, had once run along the whole south front of the building which faced the brook, and formed a pleasant and commodious walk in the open air. It was now in some places deprived of the balustrade, in others broken and narrowed; but, ruinous as it was, could still be used as a pleasant promenade. Here then walked the two ancient dames, busied in their private conversation; yet not so much so, but that Roland could observe the matrons, as their thin forms darkened the casement in passing or repassing before it, dart a glance into the apartment to see how matters were going on there.

Catherine was at the happy age of innocence and buoyancy of spirit, when, after the first moment of embarrassment was over, a situation of awkwardness like that in which she was suddently left to make acquaintance with a handsome youth, not even known to her by name, struck her, in spite of herself, in a ludicrous point of view. She bent her beautiful eyes upon the work with which she was busied, and with infinite gravity sat out the two first turns of the matrons upon the balcony; but then glancing her deep blue eye a little towards Roland, and observing the embarrassment under which he laboured, now shifting on his chair, and now dangling his cap, the whole man evincing that he was perfectly at a loss how to open the conversation, she could keep her composure no longer, but after a vain

struggle broke out into a sincere, though a very involuntary fit
of laughing, so richly accompanied by the laughter of her merry
eyes, which actually glanced through the tears which the effort
filled them with, and by the waving of her rich tresses, that the
goddess of smiles herself never looked more lovely than Catherine at that moment. A court page would not have left her
long alone in her mirth; but Roland was country-bred, and, besides, having some jealousy, as well as bashfulness, he took it
into his head that he himself was the object of her inextinguish-
able laughter. His endeavors to sympathize with Catherine,
therefore, could carry him no farther than a forced giggle, which
had more of displeasure than of mirth in it, and which so much
enhanced that of the girl, that it seemed to render it impossible
for her ever to bring her laughter to an end, with whatever anxious pains she labored to do so.

Roland sat, with some impatience, until Catherine had exhausted either her power or her desire of laughing, and was returning with good grace to the exercise of her needle, and then
he observed with some dryness, that "there seemed no great
occasion to recommend to them to improve their acquaintance,
as it seemed that they were already tolerably familiar."

Catherine had an extreme desire to set off upon a fresh score,
but she repressed it strongly, and fixing her eyes on her work,
replied by asking his pardon, and promising to avoid future
offence.

Roland had sense enough to feel that an air of offended dignity was very much misplaced, and that it was with a very different bearing he ought to meet the deep blue eyes which had
borne such a hearty burden in the laughing scene. He tried,
therefore, to extricate himself as well as he could from his blun-
der, by assuming a tone of corresponding gayety, and requesting

to know of the nymph, "how it was her pleasure that they should proceed in improving the acquaintance which had commenced so merrily."

"That," she said, "you must yourself discover; perhaps I have gone a step too far in opening our interview."

"Suppose," said Roland Græme, "we should begin as in a tale-book, by asking each other's names and histories."

"It is right well imagined," said Catherine, "and shows an argute judgment. Do you begin, and I will listen, and only put in a question or two at the dark parts of the story, Come, unfold, then, your name and history, my new acquaintance."

"I am called Roland Græme, and that tall old woman is my grandmother."

"And your tutoress?—Good. Who are your parents?"

"They are both dead," replied Roland.

"Ay, but who were they? You *had* parents, I presume?"

"I suppose so," said Roland, "but I have never been able to learn much of their history. My father was a Scottish knight, who died gallantly in his stirrups—my mother was a Græme of Heathergill, in the Debateable Land—most of her family were killed when the Debateable country was burned by the Lord Maxwell and Herries of Caerlaverock."

"Is it long ago?" said the damsel.

"Before-I was born," answered the page.

"That must be a great while since," said she, shaking her head gravely; "look you, I cannot weep for them."

"It needs not," said the youth, "they fell with honor."

"So much for your lineage, fair sir," replied his companion, "of whom I like the living specimen" (a glance at the casement) "far less than those that are dead. Your much honored grandmother looks as if she could make one weep in sad earnest.

And now, fair sir, for your own person—if you tell not the tale faster, it will be cut short in the middle ; Mother Bridget pauses longer and longer every time she passes the window, and with her there is as little mirth as in the grave of your ancestors."

" My tale is soon told : I was introduced into the Castle of Avenel to be page to the lady of the mansion, and learned to fly a hawk, halloo to a hound, back a horse, and wield lance, bow, and brand."

" And to boast of all this when you have learned it," said Catherine, " which, in France at least, is the surest accomplishment of a page.—Nay, but keep your distance, most gallant sir," said the blue-eyed maiden, as Roland edged his chair nearer to her, " for, unless I greatly mistake, these reverend ladies will soon interrupt our amicable conference, if the acquaintance they recommend shall seem to proceed beyond a certain point—so, fair sir, be pleased to abide by your station, and reply to my questions.—What might have been the unhappy event which deprived the Castle of Avenel of an inmate altogether so estimable ? "

" Truly, fair gentlewoman," answered the youth, " your real proverb says that the longest lane will have a turning, and mine was more—it was, in fine, a turning-off."

" Good ! " said the merry young maiden, " it is an apt play on the word.—And what occasion was taken for so important a catastrophe ?—Nay, start not for my learning, I do know the schools—in plain phrase, why were you sent from service ? "

The page shrugged his shoulders, while he replied: " A short tale is soon heard—and a short horse soon curried. I made the falconer's boy taste of my switch—the falconer threatened to make me brook his cudgel,—he is a kindly clown, as well as a stout, and I would rather have been cudgelled by him than any man in Christendom to choose—but I knew not his qualities at that time—so I threatened to make him brook the stab, and my Lady made me brook the 'Begone;' so adieu to the page's office and the fair Castle of Avenel. I had not travelled far before I met my venerable parent—And so tell your tale, fair gentlewoman, for mine is done."

"A happy grandmother," said the maiden, "who had the luck to find the stray page just when his mistress had slipped his leash, and a most lucky page that has jumped at once from a page to an old lady's gentleman-usher!"

"All this is nothing of your history," answered Roland Græme, who began to be much interested in the congenial vivacity of this facetious young gentlewoman,—"tale for tale is fellow-traveller's justice."

"Wait till we are fellow-travellers, then," replied Catherine.

"Nay, you escape me not so," said the page; "if you deal not justly by me, I will call out to Dame Bridget, or whatever your dame be called, and proclaim you for a cheat."

"You shall not need," answered the maiden—"my history is the counterpart of your own; the same words might almost serve, change but dress and name. I am called Catherine Seyton, and I also am an orphan."

"Have your parents been long dead?"

"That is the only question," said she, throwing down her fine eyes with a sudden expression of sorrow,—"that is the only question I cannot laugh at."

"And Dame Bridget is your grandmother?"

The sudden cloud passed away like that which crosses for an instant the summer sun, and she answered, with her usual lively expression, "Worse, by twenty degrees—Dame Bridget is my maiden aunt."

"Over gods forebode!" said Roland—"Alas! that you have such a tale to tell! And what horror comes next?"

"Your own history, exactly. I was taken upon trial for service"——

"And turned off for pinching the duenna, or affronting my lady's waiting-woman?"

"Nay, our history varies there," said the damsel—"Our mistress broke up house, or had her house broke up, which is the same thing, and I am a free woman of the forest."

"And I am as glad of it as if any one had lined my doublet with cloth of gold," said the youth. "What say you, Catherine," he continued, "if we two, thus strangely turned out of service at the same time, should give our two most venerable duennas the torch to hold, while we walk a merry measure with each other over the floor of this weary world?"

"A goodly proposal, truly," said Catherine, "and worthy the madcap brain of a discarded page!—And what shifts does your worship propose we should live by?—by singing ballads, cutting purses, or swaggering on the highway? for there, I think, you would find your most productive exchequer."

"Choose, you proud peat!" said the page, drawing off in huge disdain at the calm and unembarrassed ridicule with which his wild proposal was received. And as he spoke the words, the casement was again darkened by the forms of the matrons—it opened, and admitted Magdalen Græme and the Mother Abbess, so we must now style her, into the apartment.

JANET FOSTER.

"O, I have nought to complain of," answered the lady, "so he discharges his task with fidelity to you; and his daughter Janet is the kindest and best companion of my solitude—her little air of precision sits so well upon her!"

"Is she, indeed?" said the Earl; "she who gives you pleasure must not pass unrewarded. Come hither, damsel."

"Janet," said the lady, "come hither to my lord."

Janet, who, as we already noticed, had discreetly retired to some distance, that her presence might be no check upon the private conversation of her lord and lady, now came forward; and as she made her reverential courtesy, the Earl could not avoid smiling at the contrast which the extreme simplicity of her dress, and the prim demureness of her looks made, with a very pretty countenance, and a pair of black eyes, that laughed in spite of their mistress's desire to look grave.

"I am bound to you, pretty damsel," said the Earl, "for the contentment which your service hath given to this lady." As he said this, he took from his finger a ring of some price, and offered it to Janet Foster, adding, "Wear this, for her sake and for mine."

18

"I am well pleased, my lord," answered Janet, demurely, "that my poor service hath gratified my lady, whom no one can draw nigh to without desiring to please; but we of the precious Master Holdforth's congregation, seek not, like the gay daughters of this world, to twine gold around our fingers, or wear stones upon our necks, like the vain women of Tyre and of Sidon."

"O, what! you are a grave professor of the precise sisterhood, pretty Mrs. Janet," said the Earl, "and I think your father is of the same congregation in sincerity? I like you both the better for it; for I have been prayed for, and wished well to, in your congregations. And you may better afford the lack of ornament, Mrs. Janet, because your fingers are slender, and your neck white. But here is what neither papist nor puritan, latitudinarian nor partisan, ever boggles or makes mouths at. E'en take it, my girl, and employ it as you list."

So saying, he put into her hand five broad gold pieces of Philip and Mary.

"I would not accept this gold neither," said Janet, "but that I hope to find a use for it, which will bring a blessing on us all."

"Even please thyself, pretty Janet," said the Earl, "and I shall be well satisfied—And I prithee, let them hasten the evening collation."

AMY ROBSART,

THE Earl had re-entered the bedchamber, bent on taking a hasty farewell of the lovely Countess, and scarce daring to trust himself in private with her, to hear requests again urged which he found it difficult to parry, yet which his recent conversation with his Master of Horse had determined him not to grant.

He found her in a white cymar of silk lined with furs, her little feet unstockinged, and hastily thrust into slippers ; her un-braided hair escaping from under her midnight coif, with little array but her own loveliness.

While she stood leaning with her arms upon a table, and with a corresponding expression betwixt listlessness and expecta-tion on her fine and intelligent features, you might have searched sea and land without finding any thing half so expressive or half so lovely. The wreath of brilliants which she held did not match in lustre the hazel eye which a light brown eyebrow, pencilled with exquisite delicacy, and long eyelashes of the same color, relieved and shaded. The exercise she had lately taken, her ex-cited expectation and gratified vanity, spread a glow over her fine features, which had been sometimes censured (as beauty as well as art has her minute critics) for being rather too pale.

The milk-white pearls of the necklace which she wore, the same which she had just received as a true-love token from her husband, were excelled in purity by her teeth, and by the color of her skin, saving where the blush of pleasure and self-satisfaction had somewhat stained the neck with a shade of light crimson.

"Now, God be with thee, my dearest and loveliest!" said the Earl, scarce tearing himself from her embrace, yet again returning to fold her again and again in his arms, and again bidding farewell, and again returning to kiss and bid adieu once more. "The sun is on the verge of the blue horizon—I dare not stay. Ere this I should have been ten miles from hence."

Such were the words with which at length he strove to cut short their parting interview.

"You will not grant my request, then?" said the Countess. "Ah, false knight! did ever lady, with bare foot in slipper, seek boon of a brave knight, yet return with denial!"

"Any thing, Amy—any thing thou canst ask I will grant," answered the Earl, "always excepting," he said, "that which might ruin us both."

It was then that the Countess Amy displayed, in the midst of distresses and difficulties, the natural energy of character which would have rendered her, had fate allowed, a distinguished ornament of the rank she held. She walked up to Leicester with a composed step, a dignified air, and looks in which strong affection essayed in vain to shake the firmness of conscious truth and rectitude of principle. "Will your lordship be pleased to hear what a young and timid woman, but your most affectionate wife, can suggest in the present extremity?"

Leicester was silent, but bent his head towards the Countess, as an intimation that she was at liberty to proceed.

"There hath been but one cause for all these evils, my lord," she proceeded, "and it resolves itself into the mysterious duplicity with which you have been induced to surround yourself. Extricate yourself at once, my lord, from the tyranny of these disgraceful trammels. Be like a true English gentleman, knight, and earl, who holds that truth is the foundation of honor, and that honor is dear to him as the breath of his nostrils. Take your ill-fated wife by the hand, lead her to the footstool of Elizabeth's throne—say, that in a moment of infatuation, moved by supposed beauty, of which none perhaps can now trace even the remains, I gave my hand to this Amy Robsart. You will then have done justice to me, my lord, and to your own honor; and should law or power require you to part from me, I will oppose no objection—since I may then with honor hide a grieved and broken heart in those shades from which your love withdrew me. Then—have but a little patience, and Amy's life will not long darken your brighter prospects."

There was so much of dignity, so much of tenderness, in the Countess's remonstrance, that it moved all that was noble and generous in the soul of her husband. The scales seemed to fall from his eyes, and the duplicity and tergiversation of which he had been guilty stung him at once with remorse and shame.

"I am not worthy of you, Amy," he said, "that could weigh aught which ambition has to give against such a heart as thine! I have a bitter penance to perform, in disentangling, before sneering foes and astounded friends, all the meshes of my own deceitful policy. And the Queen—but let her take my head, as she has threatened."

"Your head, my lord!" said the Countess; "because you used the freedom and liberty of an English subject in choosing a wife? For shame; it is this distrust of the Queen's justice, this apprehension of danger, which cannot but be imaginary, that, like scarecrows, have induced you to forsake the straight-forward path, which, as it is the best, is also the safest."

MINNA TROIL.

FROM her mother, Minna inherited the stately form and
dark eyes, the raven locks and finely pencilled brows, which
showed she was, on one side at least, a stranger to the blood of
Thule.   Her cheek,—

"O call it fair, not pale!"

was so slightly and delicately tinged with the rose, that many
thought the lily had an undue proportion in her complexion.
But in that predominance of the paler flower, there was nothing
sickly or languid; it was the true natural color of health, and
corresponded in a peculiar degree with features, which seemed
calculated to express a contemplative and high-minded character.
When Minna Troil heard a tale of woe or of injustice, it was
then her blood rushed to her cheeks, and showed plainly how
warm it beat, notwithstanding the generally serious, composed,
and retiring disposition, which her countenance and demeanor
seemed to exhibit.   If strangers sometimes conceived that these
fine features were clouded by melancholy, for which her age and
situation could scarce have given occasion, they were soon satisfied, upon further acquaintance, that the placid, mild quietude

of her disposition, and the mental energy of a character which
was but little interested in ordinary and trivial occurrences, was
the real cause of her gravity; and most men, when they knew
that her melancholy had no ground in real sorrow, and was only
the aspiration of a soul bent on more important objects than
those by which she was surrounded, might have wished her
whatever could add to her happiness, but could scarce have desired that, graceful as she was in her natural and unaffected
seriousness, she should change that deportment for one more
gay. In short, notwithstanding our wish to have avoided that
hackneyed simile of an angel, we cannot avoid saying there was
something in the serious beauty of her aspect, in the measured,
yet graceful ease of her motions, in the music of her voice, and
the serene purity of her eye, that seemed as if Minna Troil belonged naturally to some higher and better sphere, and was only
the chance visitant of a world that was not worthy of her.

Minna appeared to bring to society a contented wish to be
interested and pleased with what was going forward, but her
spirit was rather placidly carried along with the stream of mirth
and pleasure, than disposed to aid its progress by any efforts of
her own. She endured mirth, rather than enjoyed it; and the
pleasures in which she most delighted, were those of a graver
and more solitary cast. The knowledge which is derived from
books was beyond her reach. Zetland afforded few opportuni-
ties in those days, of studying the lessons, bequeathed

"By dead men to their kind;"

and Magnus Troil was not a person within whose mansion the
means of such knowledge were to be acquired. But the book
of nature was before Minna, that noblest of volumes, where we

are ever called to wonder and to admire, even when we cannot understand. The plants of those wild regions, the shells on the shores, and the long list of feathered clans which haunt their cliffs and eyries, were as well known to Minna Troil as to the most experienced fowlers. Her powers of observation were wonderful, and little interrupted by other tones of feeling. The information which she acquired by habits of patient attention, was indelibly riveted in a naturally powerful memory. She had also a high feeling for the solitary and melancholy grandeur of the scenes in which she was placed. The ocean, in all its varied forms of sublimity and terror—the tremendous cliffs that resounded to the ceaseless roar of the billows, and the clang of the sea-fowl, had for Minna a charm in almost every state in which the changing seasons exhibited them. With the enthusiastic feelings proper to the romantic race from which her mother descended, the love of natural objects were to her a passion capable not only of occupying, but at times of agitating, her mind. Scenes upon which her sister looked with a sense of transient awe or emotion, which vanished on her return from witnessing them, continued long to fill Minna's imagination, not only in solitude, and in the silence of the night, but in the hours of society. So that sometimes when she sat like a beautiful statue, a present member of the domestic circle, her thoughts were far absent, wandering on the wild sea-shore, and among the yet wilder mountains of her native isles. And yet, when recalled to conversation, and mingling in it with interest, there were few to whom her friends were more indebted for enhancing its enjoyments; and although something in her manners claimed defence (notwithstanding her early youth) as well as affection, even her gay, lovely, and amiable sister was not more generally beloved than the more retired and pensive Minna.

19

Sadly, then, Brenda gazed at Minna, who sat in that rude chair of dark stone, her finely formed shape and limbs making the strongest contrast with its ponderous and irregular angles, her cheek and lips as pale as clay, and her eyes turned upward, and lighted with the mixture of resignation and excited enthusiasm, which belonged to her disease and her character. From her she looked to Norna, who muttered to herself in a low monotonous manner, as gliding from one place to another, she collected different articles, which she placed one by one on the table. And lastly, Brenda looked anxiously to her father, to gather, if possible, from his countenance, whether he entertained any part of her own fears for the consequences of the scene, considering the state of Minna's health and spirits.

MARGARET RAMSAY.

IN the sad task of examining on the walls, the written miseries of his predecessors in captivity, Lord Glenvarloch was interrupted by the sudden opening of the door of his prison-room.
It was the warder, who came to inform him, that, by order of
the Lieutenant of the Tower, his lordship was to have the society and attendance of a fellow-prisoner in his place of confinement. Nigel replied hastily, that he wished no attendance, and
would rather be left alone ; but the warder gave him to understand, with a kind of grumbling civility, that the Lieutenant
was the best judge how his prisoners should be accommodated,
and that he would have no trouble with the boy, who was
such a slip of a thing as was scarce worth turning a key upon.
—"There, Giles," he said, " bring the child in."
Another warder put the "lad before him" into the room,
and, both withdrawing, bolt crashed and chain clanged, as they
replaced these ponderous obstacles to freedom. The boy was
clad in a gray suit of the finest cloth, laid down with silver lace,
with a buff-colored cloak of the same pattern. His cap, which

was a Montero of black velvet, was pulled over his brows, and, with the profusion of his long ringlets, almost concealed his face. He stood on the very spot where the warder had quitted his collar, about two steps from the door of the apartment, his eyes fixed on the ground, and every joint trembling with confusion and terror. Nigel could well have dispensed with his society, but it was not in his nature to behold distress, whether of body or mind, without endeavoring to relieve it.

"Cheer up," he said, "my pretty lad. We are to be companions, it seems, for a little time—at least I trust your confinement will be short, since you are too young to have done aught to deserve long restraint."

The boy suffered himself to be led and seated by the fire, but, after retaining for a long time the very posture which he assumed in sitting down, he suddenly changed it in order to wring his hands with an air of the bitterest distress, and then, spreading them before his face, wept so plentifully, that the tears found their way in floods through his slender fingers.

"Tell me who and what you are, my pretty boy," said Nigel. "Consider me, child, as a companion, who wishes to be kind to you, would you but teach him how he can be so."

"Sir—my lord, I mean," answered the boy, very timidly, and in a voice which could scarce be heard even across the brief distance which divided them, "you are very good—and I—am very unhappy"—

"There is something singular about you, my young friend," said Lord Glenvarloch, withdrawing with a gentle degree of compulsion the hand with which the boy had again covered his eyes ; "do not pain yourself with thinking on your situation just at present—your pulse is high, and your hand feverish—lay yourself on yonder pallet, and try to compose yourself to sleep. It is the readiest and best remedy for the fancies with which you are worrying yourself."

"I thank you for your considerate kindness, my lord," said the boy ; "with your leave I will remain for a little space quiet in this chair—I am better thus than on the couch. I can think undisturbedly on what I have done, and have still to do ; and if God sends slumber to a creature so exhausted, it shall be most welcome."

So saying, the boy drew his hand from Lord Nigel's, and, drawing around him and partly over his face the folds of his ample cloak, he resigned himself to sleep or meditation, while his companion, notwithstanding the exhausting scenes of this and the preceding day, continued his pensive walk up and down the apartment.

Every reader has experienced, that times occur, when, far from being lords of external circumstances, man is unable to rule even the wayward realm of his own thoughts. It was Nigel's natural wish to consider his own situation coolly, and fix on the course which it became him as a man of sense and courage to adopt ; and yet, in spite of himself, and notwithstanding the deep-interest of the critical state in which he was placed, it did so happen that his fellow-prisoner's situation occupied more of his thoughts than did his own. There was no accounting for this wandering of the imagination, but also there was no striving with it. The pleading tones of one of the sweetest voices he had ever heard, still rung in his ear, though it seemed that sleep had now fettered the tongue of the speaker. He drew nearer on tiptoe to satisfy himself whether it were so. The folds of the cloak hid the lower part of his face entirely ; but the bon-net, which had fallen a little aside, permitted him to see the forehead streaked with blue veins, the closed eyes, and the long silken eyelashes.

"Poor child," said Nigel to himself, as he looked on him, nestled up as it were in the folds of his mantle, "the dew is yet on thy eyelashes, and thou hast fairly wept thyself asleep. Sor-row is a rough nurse to one so young and delicate as thou art. Peace be to thy slumbers, I will not disturb them. My own misfortunes require my attention, and it is to their contemplation that I must resign myself."

The harsh sound of the revolving bolts was again heard, and the voice of the warder announced that a man desired to speak with Lord Glenvarloch.

"Soh!" said Nigel, something displeased, "I find even a prison does not save one from importunate visitations."

The door opened, and the worthy citizen, George Heriot, entered the prison-chamber.

He cast around the apartment his usual sharp, quick glance of observation, and, advancing to Nigel, said : "My lord, I wish I could say I was happy to see you."

"The sight of those who are unhappy themselves, Master Heriot, seldom produces happiness to their friends—I, however, am glad to see you."

"My lord, why do I find you in this place, and whelmed with charges which must blacken a name rendered famous by ages of virtue ? "

"Simply, then, you find me here," said Nigel, "because, to begin from my original error, I would be wiser than my father."

"It is well, my lord," answered Heriot, coldly. " You have

a right, such as it is, to keep your own secrets; but, since my
discourse on these points seems so totally unavailing, we had
better proceed to business.   Yet your father's image rises before
me, and seems to plead that I should go on."

"Be it as you will, sir," said Glenvarloch.

"You cannot have forgotten, my lord," said Heriot, "the
transaction which took place some weeks since at Lord Hunting-
len's, by which a large sum of money was advanced for the re-
demption of your lordship's estate?"

"I remember it perfectly," said Nigel.

Heriot bowed gravely, and went on.   "That money was advanced under the expectation and hope that it might be replaced
by the contents of a grant to your lordship, under the royal sign-
manual, in payment of certain moneys due by the crown to your
father.   I trust your lordship understood the transaction at the
time.—I trust you now understand my resumption of its import,
and hold it to be correct?"

"Undeniably correct," answered Lord Glenvarloch.   "If
the sums contained in the warrant cannot be recovered, my lands
become the property of those who paid off the original holders
of the mortgage, and now stand in their right."

"If you will trust me with the warrant under the sign-man-
ual, I believe circumstances do now so stand at Court, that I
may be able to recover the money for you."

"I would do so gladly," said Lord Glenvarloch, "but the
casket which contains it is not in my possession.   It was seized
when I was arrested at Greenwich."

"It will be no longer withheld from you," said Heriot;
"your baggage was in the little ante-room as I passed—the casket caught my eye—you had it of me.   Ho! warder, bring in
Lord Glenvarloch's baggage."   The officer obeyed.   Seals had

been placed upon the trunk and casket, but were now removed, the warder said, in consequence of the subsequent orders from Court, and the whole was placed at the prisoner's free disposal.

Desirous to bring this painful visit to a conclusion, Lord Glenvarloch opened the casket, and looked through the papers which it contained, first hastily, and then more slowly and accurately; but it was all in vain. The Sovereign's signed warrant had disappeared.

"I thought and expected nothing better," said George Heriot, bitterly. "The beginning of evil is the letting out of water. Here is a fair heritage lost, I dare say, on a foul cast at dice, or a conjuring trick at cards!—My lord, your surprise is well played. I give you full joy of your accomplishments. I have seen many as young brawlers and spendthrifts, but never so young and accomplished a dissembler. Nay, man, never bend your angry brows on me. I speak in bitterness of heart, from what I remember of your worthy father; and if his son hears of his degeneracy from no one else, he shall hear of it from the old goldsmith."

This new suspicion drove Nigel to the very extremity of his patience; yet the motives and zeal of the good old man, as well as the circumstances of suspicion which created his displeasure, were so excellent an excuse for it, that they formed an absolute curb on the resentment of Lord Glenvarloch, and constrained him, after two or three hasty exclamations, to observe a proud and sullen silence. At length, Master Heriot resumed his lecture.

"Hark you, my lord," he said, "it is scarce possible that this most important paper can be absolutely assigned away.

Let me know in what obscure corner, and for what petty sum, it lies pledged—something may yet be done."

" Your efforts in my favor are the more generous," said Lord Glenvarloch, " as you offer them to one whom you believe you have cause to think hardly of—but they are altogether unavailing. Fortune has taken the field against me at every point. Even let her win the battle."

" Zouns!" exclaimed Heriot, impatiently ; " you would make a saint swear! Why, I tell you, if this paper, the loss of which seems to sit so light on you, be not found, farewell to the fair lordship of Glenvarloch—firth and forest—lea and furrow— lake and stream—all that has been in the house of Olifaunt since the days of William the Lion! "

" Farewell to them, then," said Nigel, " and that moan is soon made."

" 'Sdeath! my lord, you will make more moan for it ere you die," said Heriot, in the same tone of angry impatience.

" Not I, my old friend," said Nigel. " If I mourn, Master Heriot, it will be for having lost the good opinion of a worthy man, and lost it, as I must say, most undeservedly."

" Ay, ay, young man," said Heriot, shaking his head, " make me believe that if you can. To sum the matter up," he said, rising from his seat, and walking towards that occupied by the disguised female, " for our matters are now drawn into small compass, you shall as soon make me believe that this masquerading mummy, on whom I now lay the hand of paternal authority, is a French page, who understands no English."

So saying, he took hold of the supposed page's cloak, and not without some gentle degree of violence, led into the middle

20

of the apartment the disguised fair one, who in vain attempted to cover her face, first with her mantle, and afterwards with her hands; both which impediments Master Heriot removed, somewhat unceremoniously, and gave to view the detected daughter of the old horologist, his own fair god-daughter, Margaret Ramsay.

ALICE BRIDGENORTH.

As he approached the monument of Goddard Crovan, Julian cast many an anxious glance to see whether any object visible beside the huge gray stone, should apprise him whether he was anticipated, at the appointed place of rendezvous, by her who had named it. Nor was it long before the flutter of a mantle, which the breeze slightly waved, and the motion necessary to re-place it upon the wearer's shoulders, made him aware that Alice had already reached their place of meeting. One instant set the palfrey at liberty, with slackened girths and loosened reins, to pick its own way through the dell at will; another placed Julian Peveril by the side of Alice Bridgenorth.

A lovely girl—bred in solitude, and in the quiet and unpre-tending tastes which solitude encourages—spirited also and in-quisitive, and listening, with a laughing cheek and an eager eye, to every tale which the young angler brought from the town and castle. The sad-colored gown—the pinched and plaited cap, which carefully obscured the profusion of long dark-brown hair —the small ruff, and the long sleeves, would have appeared to great disadvantage on a shape less graceful than Alice Bridge-north's; but an exquisite form, though not, as yet, sufficiently rounded in the outlines to produce the perfection of female beauty, was able to sustain and give grace even to this unbecoming dress. Her countenance, fair and delicate, with eyes of hazel, and a brow of alabaster, had, notwithstanding, less regular beauty than her form, and might have been justly subjected to criticism. There was, however, a life and spirit in her gayety, and a depth of sentiment in her gravity, which made Alice, in conversation with the very few persons with whom she associated, so fascinating in her manners and expression, whether of language or countenance—so touching, also, in her simplicity and purity of thought, that brighter beauties might have been overlooked in her company. It was no wonder, therefore, that an ardent character like Julian, influenced by these charms, as well as by the secrecy and mystery attending his intercourse with Alice, should prefer the recluse of the Black Fort to all others with whom he had become acquainted in general society.

That Alice should extend her hand to her lover, as with the ardor of a young greyhound he bounded over the obstacles of the rugged path, was as natural as that Julian, seizing on the hand so kindly stretched out, should devour it with kisses, and, for a moment or two, without reprehension; while the other hand, which should have aided in the liberation of its fellow, served to hide the blushes of the fair owner. But Alice, young as she was, and attached to Julian by such long habits of kindly intimacy, still knew well how to subdue the tendency of her own treacherous affections.

It required but a few energetic words for Julian to explain to Alice at once his feelings, and to make her sensible of the real nature of her own. She wept plentifully, but her tears were not all of bitterness. She sat passively still, and without reply, while he explained to her, with many an interjection, the

circumstances which had placed discord between their families ;
for hitherto, all that she had known was, that Master Peveril,
belonging to the household of the great Countess or Lady of
Man, must observe some precautions in visiting a relative of the
unhappy Colonel Christian. But, when Julian concluded his
tale with the warmest protestations of eternal love, "My poor
father !" she burst forth, " and was this to be the end of all thy
precautions ?—This, that the son of him that disgraced and
banished thee, should hold such language to your daughter !"

" You err, Alice, you err," cried Julian, eagerly. " That I
hold this language—that the son of Peveril addresses thus the
daughter of your father—that he thus kneels to you for forgiveness of injuries which passed when we were both infants, shows
the will of Heaven, that in our affection should be quenched the
discord of our parents. What else could lead those who parted
infants on the hills of Derbyshire, to meet thus in the valleys
of Man ? "

Alice, however new such a scene, and, above all, her own
emotions, might be, was highly endowed with that exquisite
delicacy which is imprinted in the female heart, to give warning
of the slightest approach to impropriety in a situation like hers.

" Rise, rise, Master Peveril," she said ; " do not do yourself
and me this injustice—we have done both wrong—very wrong ;
but my fault was done in ignorance. Oh God ! my poor father,
who needs comfort so much—is it for me to add to his misfortunes ?—Rise ! " she added, more firmly ; "if you retain this
unbecoming posture any longer, I will leave the room, and you
shall never see me more."

The commanding tone of Alice overawed the impetuosity of
her lover, who took in silence a seat removed to some distance
from hers, and was again about to speak. " Julian," she said,

in a milder tone, "you have spoken enough, and more than
enough. Would you had left me in the pleasing dream in
which I could have listened to you forever! but the hour of
wakening is arrived." Peveril waited the prosecution of her
speech as a criminal while he waits his doom; for he was sufficiently sensible that an answer, delivered not certainly without
emotion, but with firmness and resolution, was not to be interrupted. "We have done wrong," she repeated, "very wrong;
and if we now separate forever, the pain we may feel will be
but a just penalty for our error. We should never have met.
Meeting, we should part as soon as possible. Our farther intercourse can but double our pain at parting.—Farewell, Julian;
and forget we ever have seen each other!"

"Forget!" said Julian; "never, never. To *you* it is easy
to speak the word—to think the thought. To *me*, an approach
to either can only be by utter destruction."

JACQUELINE.

"Blaspheme not the Saints, my young friend," said Maitre Pierre. "Saint Julian is the faithful patron of travellers; and, peradventure, the blessed Saint Quentin had done more and better for thee than thou art aware of."

As he spoke, the door opened, and a girl, rather above than under fifteen years old, entered with a platter covered with damask, on which was placed a small saucer of the dried plums which have always added to the reputation of Tours, and a cup of the curiously chased plate which the goldsmiths of that city were anciently famous for executing with a delicacy of workmanship that distinguished them from the other cities of France, and even excelled the skill of the metropolis. The form of the goblet was so elegant, that Durward thought not of observing closely whether the material was of silver, or, like what had been placed before himself, of a baser metal, but so well burnished as to resemble the richer ore.

But the sight of the young person by whom this service was executed, attracted Durward's attention far more than the petty minutiæ of the duty which she performed.

He speedily made the discovery, that a quantity of long black

tresses, which, in the maiden fashion of his own country, were
unadorned by any ornament, except a single chaplet lightly
woven out of ivy leaves, formed a veil around a countenance,
which, in its regular features, dark eyes, and pensive expression,
resembled that of Melpomene, though there was a faint glow on
the cheek, and an intelligence on the lips and in the eye, which
made it seem that gayety was not foreign to a countenance so
expressive, although it might not be its most habitual expression.
Quentin even thought he could discern that depressing circumstances were the cause why a countenance so young and so
lovely was graver than belongs to early beauty; and as the romantic imagination of youth is rapid in drawing conclusions
from slight premises, he was pleased to infer, from what follows,
that the fate of this beautiful vision was wrapped in silence and
mystery.

" How now, Jacqueline ! " said Maitre Pierre, when she en-
tered the apartment,—" Wherefore this ?   Did I not desire that
Dame Perette should bring what I wanted ?—*Pasques-dieu !*—
Is she, or does she think herself, too good to serve me ? "

" My kinswoman is ill at ease," answered Jacqueline, in a
hurried yet an humble tone; "ill at ease, and keeps her chamber."

" She keeps it *alone*, I hope ? " replied Maitre Pierre, with
some emphasis; " I am *vieux routier*, and none of those upon
whom feigned disorders pass for apologies."

Jacqueline turned pale, and even tottered at the answer of
Maitre Pierre; for it must be owned, that his voice and looks,
at all times harsh, caustic, and unpleasing, had, when he expressed anger or suspicion, an effect both sinister and alarming.

The mountain chivalry of Quentin Durward was instantly
awakened, and he hastened to approach Jacqueline, and relieve

her of the burden she bore, and which she passively resigned to
him, while with a timid and anxious look, she watched the countenance of the angry burgess. It was not in nature to resist the
piercing and pity-craving expression of her looks, and Maitre
Pierre proceeded, not merely with an air of diminished displeasure, but with as much gentleness as he could assume in countenance and manner, " I blame not thee, Jacqueline, and thou art
too young to be—what it is pity to think thou must be one day
—a false and treacherous thing, like the rest of thy giddy sex.
No man ever lived to man's estate, but he had the opportunity
to know you all. Here is a Scottish cavalier will tell you the
same."

Jacqueline looked for an instant on the young stranger, as
if to obey Maitre Pierre, but the glance, momentary as it was,
appeared to Durward a pathetic appeal to him for support and
sympathy; and with the promptitude dictated by the feelings
of youth, and the romantic veneration for the female sex inspired
by his education, he answered hastily, " That he would throw
down his gage to any antagonist, of equal rank and equal age,
who should presume to say such a countenance as that which he
now looked upon, could be animated by other than the purest
and the truest mind."

The young woman grew deadly pale, and cast an apprehensive glance upon Maitre Pierre, in whom the bravado of the
young gallant seemed only to excite laughter, more scornful than
applausive Quentin, whose second thoughts generally corrected
the first, though sometimes after they had found utterance,
blushed deeply at having uttered what might be construed into
an empty boast, in presence of an old man of a peaceful profession; and, as a sort of just and appropriate penance, resolved
patiently to submit to the ridicule which he had incurred. He

21

offered the cup and trencher to Maitre Pierre with a blush in his cheek, and a humiliation of countenance which endeavored to disguise itself under an embarrassed smile.

"You are a foolish young man," said Maitre Pierre, "and know as little of women as of princes—whose hearts," he said, crossing himself devoutly, "God keeps in his right hand."

"And who keeps those of the women, then?" said Quentin, resolved, if he could help it, not to be borne down by the assumed superiority of this extraordinary old man, whose lofty and careless manner possessed an influence over him of which he felt ashamed.

"I am afraid you must ask of them in another quarter," said Maitre Pierre, composedly.

THE UNKNOWN.

FATHER BUONAVENTURE extended his hand towards Alan, who was about to pledge his faith in the usual form by grasping it with his own, when the Father drew back hastily. Ere Alan had time to comment upon this repulse, a small side-door, covered with tapestry, was opened; the hangings were drawn aside, and a lady, as if by sudden apparition, glided into the apartment. It was neither of the Miss Arthurets, but a woman in the prime of life, and in the full-blown expansion of female beauty, tall, fair, and commanding in her aspect. Her locks, of paly gold, were taught to fall over a brow, which, with the stately glance of the large, open, blue eyes, might have become Juno herself; her neck and bosom were admirably formed, and of a dazzling whiteness. She was rather inclined to *embonpoint*, but not more than became her age, of apparently thirty years. Her step was that of a queen, but it was of Queen Vashti, not Queen Esther—the bold and commanding, not the retiring beauty.

Father Buonaventure raised himself on the couch, angrily, as if displeased by this intrusion. " How now, madam," he said, with some sternness ; " why have we the honor of your company ? "

" Because it is my pleasure," answered the lady, composedly.

" Your pleasure, madame ! " he repeated in the same angry tone.

" My pleasure, sir," she continued, " which always keeps exact pace with my duty.   I had heard you were unwell—let me hope it is only business which produces this seclusion."

" I am well," he replied ; " perfectly well, and I thank you for your care—but we are not alone, and this young man "——

" That young man ? " she said, bending her large and serious eye on Alan Fairford, as if she had been for the first time aware of his presence—" may I ask who he is ? "

" Another time, madame ; you shall learn his history after he is gone."

" After he is gone may be too late," said the lady.

" Peace, madame," said Father Buonaventure, rising up ; " be silent, or quit the apartment ; my designs do not admit of female criticism."

To this peremptory command the lady seemed about to make a sharp reply ; but she checked herself, and pressing her lips strongly together, as if to secure the words from bursting from them which were already formed upon her tongue, she made a deep reverence, partly as it seemed in reproach, partly in respect, and left the room as suddenly as she had entered it.

GREENMANTLE.

ALAN FAIRFORD was in the act of speaking to the masked lady, (for Miss Redgauntlet had retained her riding vizard,) endeavoring to assure her as he perceived her anxiety, of such protection as he could afford, when his own name, pronounced in a loud tone, attracted his attention. He looked round, and, seeing Peter Peebles, as hastily turned to avoid his notice, in which he succeeded, so earnest was Peter upon his colloquy with one of the most respectable auditors whose attention he had ever been able to engage. And by this little motion, momentary as it was, Alan gained an unexpected advantage; for while he looked round, Miss Lilias, I could never ascertain why, took the moment to adjust her mask, and did it so awkwardly, that when her companion again turned his head, he recognized as much of her features as authorized him to address her as his fair client, and to press his offers of protection and assistance with the boldness of a former acquaintance.

Lilias Redgauntlet withdrew the mask from her crimsoned cheek. "Mr. Fairford," she said, in a voice almost inaudible, "you have the character of a young gentleman of sense and generosity; but we have already met in one situation which you must think singular; and I must be exposed to misconstruction, at least for my forwardness, were it not in a cause in which my dearest affections were concerned."

"Any interest in my beloved friend, Darsie Latimer," said Fairford, stepping a little back, and putting a marked restraint upon his former advances, "gives me a double right to be useful to"— He stopped short.

"To his sister, your goodness would say," answered Lilias.

"His sister, madame!" replied Alan, in the extremity of astonishment—"Sister, I presume in affection only?"

"No, sir; my dear brother Darsie and I are connected by the bonds of actual relationship; and I am not sorry to be the first to tell this to the friend he most values."

Fairford's first thought was on the violent passion which Darsie had expressed towards the fair unknown. "Good God!" he exclaimed, "how did he bear the discovery?"

"With resignation, I hope," said Lilias, smiling. "A more accomplished sister he might easily have come by, but scarcely could have found one who could love him more than I do."

"I meant—I only meant to say," said the young counsellor, his presence of mind failing him for an instant—"that is, I meant to ask where Darsie Latimer is at this moment."

"In this very house, and under the guardianship of his uncle, whom I believe you knew as a visitor of your father, under the name of Mr. Herries of Birrenswork."

"Let me hasten to him," said Fairford; "I have sought him through difficulties and dangers—I must see him instantly."

"You forget you are a prisoner," said the young lady.

"True—true; but I cannot be long detained—the cause alleged is too ridiculous."

"Alas!" said Lilias, "our fate—my brother's and mine, at

least—must turn on the deliberations perhaps of less than an hour. For you, sir, I believe and apprehend nothing but some restraint; my uncle is neither cruel nor unjust, though few will go farther in the course which he has adopted."

" Which is that of the Pretend—"

" For God's sake speak lower!" said Lilias, approaching her hand, as if to stop him. " The word may cost you your life. You do not know—indeed you do not—the terrors of the situation in which we at present stand, and in which I fear you also are involved by your friendship for my brother."

" I do not indeed know the particulars of our situation," said Fairford; " but be the danger what it may I shall not grudge my share of it for the sake of my friend; or," he added, with more timidity, " of my friend's sister. Let me hope," he said, " my dear Miss Latimer, that my presence may be of some use to you; and that it may be so let me entreat a share of your confidence, which I am conscious I have otherwise no right to ask."

He led her, as he spoke, towards the recess of the farther window of the room, and observing to her that, unhappily, he was particularly exposed to interruption from the mad old man whose entrance had alarmed her, he disposed of Darsie Latimer's riding-skirt, which had been left in the apartment, over the back of two chairs, forming thus a sort of screen, behind which he ensconced himself with the maiden of the green-mantle; feeling at the moment, that the danger in which he was placed was almost compensated by the intelligence which permitted those feelings towards her to revive, which justice to his friend had induced him to stifle in the birth.

The relative situation of adviser and advised, of protector and protected, is so peculiarly suited to the respective condition
22

of man and woman, that great progress towards intimacy is
often made in very short space ; for the circumstances call for
confidence on the part of the gentleman, and forbid coyness on
that of the lady, so that the usual barriers against easy intercourse are at once thrown down.

Under these circumstances, securing themselves as far as
possible from observation, conversing in whispers, and seated
in a corner, where they were brought into so close contact that
their faces nearly touched each other, Fairford heard from Lilias
Redgauntlet the history of her family, particularly of her uncle ;
his views upon her brother, and the agony which she felt, lest at
that very moment he might succeed in engaging Darsie in some
desperate scheme, fatal to his fortune, and perhaps to his life.

RACHAEL GEDDES.

In a few minutes after Mr. Geddes had concluded the account of himself and his family, his sister Rachael, the only surviving member of it, entered the room. Her appearance is remarkably pleasing, and although her age is certainly thirty at least, she still retains the shape and motion of an earlier period. The absence of every thing like fashion or ornament was, as usual, atoned for by the most perfect neatness and cleanliness of her dress ; and her simple close cap was particularly suited to eyes which had the softness and simplicity of the dove's. Her features were also extremely agreeable, but had suffered a little through the ravages of that professed enemy to beauty, the small-pox ; a disadvantage which was in part counterbalanced by a well-formed mouth, teeth like pearls, and a pleasing sobriety of smile, that seemed to wish good here and hereafter to every one she spoke to. You cannot make any of your vile inferences here, Alan, for I have given a full-length picture of Rachael Geddes ; so that you cannot say in this case, as in the letter I have just received, that she was passed over as a subject on which I feared to dilate. More of this anon.

You know, Alan, how easily I am determined by any thing

resembling cordiality—and so, though a little afraid of the formality of my host and hostess, I accepted their invitation provided I could get some messenger to send to Shepherd's Bush for my servant and portmanteau.

"Why, truly, friend," said Joshua, "thine outward frame would be improved by cleaner garments; but I will do thine errand myself to the Widow Gregson's house of reception, and send thy lad hither with thy clothes. Meanwhile Rachael will show thee these little gardens, and then will put thee in some way of spending thy time usefully, till our meal calls us together at the second hour afternoon. I bid thee farewell for the present, having some space to walk, seeing I must leave the animal Solomon to his refreshing rest."

With these words, Mr. Joshua Geddes withdrew. Some ladies we have known would have felt, or at least affected, reserve or embarrassment, at being left to do the honors of the grounds to—(it will be out, Alan)—a smart young fellow—an entire stranger. She went out for a few minutes, and returned in her plain cloak and bonnet, with her beaver-gloves, prepared to act as my guide, with as much simplicity as if she had been to wait upon thy father. So forth I sallied with my fair Quaker.

ROSE FLAMMOCK.

Rose Flammock, the daughter of Wilkin, a blue-eyed Flemish maiden, round, plump, and shy as a partridge, who had been for some time permitted to keep company with the high-born Norman damsel, in a doubtful station, betwixt that of an humble friend and superior domestic.

Berwine now exhorted her as she valued her life, to retire into the first anteroom, where the beds were prepared, and betake herself, if not to rest, at least to silence and devotion; but the faithful Flemish girl stoutly refused her entreaties, and resisted her commands.

" Talk not to me of danger," she said; " here I remain, that I may be at least within hearing of my mistress's danger, and woe betide those who shall offer her injury! Take notice, that twenty Norman spears surround this inhospitable dwelling, prompt to avenge whatsoever injury shall be offered to the daughter of Raymond Berenger."

"Reserve your threats for those who are mortal," said Berwine, in a low, but piercing whisper; "the owner of yonder chamber fears them not. Farewell—thy danger be on thine own head!"

She departed, leaving Rose strangely agitated by what had passed, and somewhat appalled at her last words. " I will see," said the maiden, " if the Normans are on their post, since it is to them I must trust, if a moment of need should arrive."

Thus reflecting, Rose Flammock went to the window of the little apartment, in order to satisfy herself of the vigilance of the sentinels, and to ascertain the exact situation of the corps de garde. The moon was at the full. From the level plain beyond, the space adjoining to the castle was in a considerable degree clear, and the moonbeams slumbered on its close and beautiful turf, mixed with long shadows of the towers and trees. Beyond this esplanade lay the forest ground, with a few gigantic oaks scattered individually along the skirt of its dark and ample domain.

The calm beauty and repose of a scene so lovely, the stillness of all around, and the more matured reflections which the whole suggested, quieted, in some measure, the apprehensions which the events of the evening had inspired. "After all," she reflected, "why should I be so anxious on account of the Lady Eveline ? There is among the proud Normans and the dogged Saxons scarce a single family of note, but must needs be held distinguished from others by some superstitious observance peculiar to their race, as if they thought it scorn to go to Heaven like a poor simple Fleming, such as I am. Could I but see a Norman sentinel, I would hold myself satisfied of my mistress's security. And yonder one stalks along the gloom, wrapped in his long white mantle, and the moon tipping the point of his lance with silver. What ho, Sir Cavalier ! "

The Norman turned his steps, and approached the ditch as she spoke. " What is your pleasure, damsel ? " he demanded.

" The window next to mine is that of Lady Eveline Berenger,

whom you are appointed to guard. Please to give needful watch upon this side of the castle."

" Doubt it not, lady," answered the cavalier; and, enveloping himself in his long *chappe*, or military watch-cloak, he withdrew to a large oak-tree at some distance, and stood there with folded arms, and leaning on his lance, more like a trophy of armour than a living warrior.

Emboldened by the consciousness, that in case of need succor was close at hand, Rose drew back into her little chamber, and having ascertained by listening that there was no noise or stirring in that of Eveline, she began to make some preparations for her own repose. For this purpose she went into the outward anteroom, where Dame Gillian, whose fears had given way to the soporiferous effects of a copious draught of *lithe-alos*, (mild ale, of the first strength and quality,) slept as sound a sleep as that generous Saxon beverage could procure.

Muttering an indignant censure on her sloth and indifference, Rose caught, from the empty couch which had been destined for her own use the upper covering, and dragging it with her into the inner anteroom, disposed it so as, with the assistance of the rushes which strewed that apartment, to form a sort of couch upon which, half seated, half reclined, she resolved to pass the night in as close attendance upon her mistress as circumstances permitted.

Thus seated, her eye on the pale planet which sailed in full glory through the blue sky of midnight, she proposed to herself that sleep should not visit her eyelids till the dawn of morning should assure her of Eveline's safety.

Her thoughts, meanwhile, rested on the boundless and shadowy world beyond the grave, and on the great and perhaps yet undecided question, whether the separation of its inhabitants from those of this temporal sphere is absolute and decided, or whether influenced by motives which we cannot appreciate, they continue to hold shadowy communication with those yet existing in earthly reality of flesh and blood? To have denied this, would, in the age of crusades and of miracles, have incurred the guilt of heresy; but Rose's firm good sense led her to doubt at least the frequency of supernatural interference, and she comforted herself with an opinion, contradicted, however, by her own involuntary starts and shudderings at every leaf which moved, that, in submitting to the performance of the rite imposed on her, Eveline incurred no real danger, and only sacrificed to an obsolete family superstition.

As this conviction strengthened on Rose's mind, her purpose of vigilance began to decline—her thoughts wandered to objects towards which they were not directed, like sheep which stray beyond the charge of their shepherd—her eyes no longer brought back to her a distinct apprehension of the broad, round, silvery orb on which they continued to gaze. At length they closed, and seated on the folded mantle, her back resting against the wall of the apartment, and her white arms folded on her bosom, Rose Flammock fell fast asleep.

EVELINE BERENGER.

"DARE I venture to hope," continued De Lacy, without taking offence at the dryness of the Abbess's manner, "that Lady Eveline has heard this most unhappy change of circumstances without emotion,—I would say, without displeasure?"

"She is the daughter of a Berenger, my lord," answered the Abbess, "and it is our custom to punish a breach of faith, or to contemn it—never to grieve over it. What my niece may do in this case I know not. I am a woman of religion, sequestered from the world, and would advise peace and Christian forgiveness, with a proper sense of contempt for the unworthy treatment which she has received. She has followers and vassals, and friends, doubtless, and advisers, who may not, in blinded zeal for worldly honor, recommend to her to sit down slightly with this injury, but desire she should rather appeal to the king, or to the arms of her father's followers, unless her liberty is restored to her by the surrender of the contract into which she has been enticed. But she comes, to answer for herself."

Eveline entered at the moment, leaning on Rose's arm. She had laid aside mourning since the ceremony of the *fiancailles*, and was dressed in a kirtle of white, with an upper robe of pale

23

blue. Her head was covered with a veil of white gauze, so thin
as to float about her like the misty cloud usually painted around
the countenance of a seraph. But the face of Eveline, though
in beauty not unworthy one of this angelic order, was at present
far from resembling that of a seraph in tranquillity of expression.
Her limbs trembled, her cheeks were pale, the tinge of red
around the eyelids expressed recent tears; yet amidst these
natural signs of distress and uncertainty, there was an air of
profound resignation—a resolution to discharge her duty in
every emergence, reigning in the solemn expression of her eye
and eyebrow, and showing her prepared to govern the agitation
which she could not entirely subdue. And so well were these
opposing qualities of timidity and resolution mingled on her
cheek, that Eveline, in the utmost pride of her beauty, never
looked more fascinating than at that instant; and Hugo de
Lacy, hitherto rather an unimpassioned lover, stood in her presence with feelings as if all the exaggerations of romance were
realized, and his mistress were a being of a higher sphere, from
whose doom he was to receive happiness or misery, life or
death.

It was under the influence of such a feeling that the warrior
dropped on one knee before Eveline, took the hand which she
rather resigned than gave to him, pressed it to his lips fervently,
and, ere he parted with it, moistened it with one of the few tears
which he was ever known to shed. But, although surprised, and
carried out of his character by a sudden impulse, he regained his
composure on observing that the Abbess regarded his humiliation, if it can be so termed, with an air of triumph; and he entered on his defence before Eveline with a manly earnestness,
not devoid of fervor, nor free from agitation, yet made in a tone

of firmness and pride, which seemed assumed to meet and control that of the offended Abbess.

"Lady," he said, addressing Eveline, "you have heard from
the venerable Abbess in what unhappy position I have been
placed since yesterday by the rigor of the Archbishop—perhaps
I should rather say by his just though severe interpretation of
my engagement in the Crusade. I cannot doubt that all this
has been stated with accurate truth by the venerable lady; bu*
as I must no longer call her my friend, let me fear whether she
has done me justice in her commentary upon the unhappy necessity which must presently compel me to leave my country,
and with my country to forego—at least to postpone—the fairest hopes which man ever entertained. The venerable lady hath
upbraided me, that being myself the cause that the execution of
yesterday's contract is postponed, I would fain keep it suspended over your head for an indefinite term of years. No one
resigns willingly such rights as yesterday gave me; and, let me
speak a boastful word, sooner than yield them up to man of
woman born, I would hold a fair field against all comers, with
girded sword and sharp spear, from sunrise to sunset, for three
days' space. But what I would retain at the price of a thousand
lives, I am willing to renounce if it would cost you a single sigh.
If, therefore, you think you cannot remain happy as the betrothed
of De Lacy, you may command my assistance to have the
contract annulled, and make some more fortunate man
happy."

He would have gone on, but felt the danger of being over-
powered again by those feelings of tenderness so new to his
steady nature, that he blushed to give way to them.

Eveline remained silent. The Abbess took the word.

"Kinswoman," she said, "you hear that the generosity, or
the justice of the Constable of Chester, proposes, in consequence
of his departure upon a distant and perilous expedition, to can-
cel a contract entered into upon the specific and precise understanding that he was to remain in England for its fulfilment.
You cannot, methinks, hesitate to accept of the freedom which
he offers you, with thanks for his bounty. For my part, I will
reserve mine own until I shall see that your joint application is
sufficient to win to your purpose his Grace of Canterbury, who
may again interfere with the actions of his friend the Lord Constable, over whom he has already exerted so much influence—
for the weal, doubtless, of his spiritual concerns."

"If it is meant by your words, venerable lady," said the
Constable, "that I have any purpose of sheltering myself behind
the Prelate's authority, to avoid doing that which I proclaim my
readiness, though not my willingness, to do, I can only say, that
you are the first who has doubted the faith of Hugh de Lacy."
And while the proud Baron thus addressed a female and a recluse, he could not prevent his eye from sparkling and his cheek
from flushing.

"My gracious and venerable kinswoman," said Eveline, sum-
moning together her resolution, "and you, my good lord, be
not offended, if I pray you not to increase by groundless suspicions and hasty resentments your difficulties and mine. My
lord, the obligations which I lie under to you are such as I can
never discharge, since they comprehend fortune, life, and honor.
Know that, in my anguish of mind, when besieged by the
Welsh in my castle of the Garde Douloureuse, I vowed to the
Virgin, that (my honor safe) I would place myself at the disposal of him whom our Lady should employ as her instrument to
relieve me from yonder hour of agony. In giving me a deliv-

erer, she gave me a master; nor could I desire a more noble one than Hugo de Lacy."

"God forbid, lady," said the Constable, speaking eagerly, as if he was afraid his resolution should fail him ere he could get the renunciation uttered, "that I should, by such a tie, to which you subjected yourself in the extremity of your distress, bind you to any resolution in my favor which can put force on your own inclinations!"

The Abbess herself could not help expressing her applause of this sentiment, declaring it was spoken like a Norman gentleman; but, at the same time, her eyes, turned towards her niece, seemed to exhort her to beware how she declined to profit by the candor of De Lacy.

But Eveline proceeded, with her eyes fixed on the ground, and a slight color overspreading her face, to state her own sentiments, without listening to the suggestions of any one. "I will own, noble sir," she said, "that when your valor had rescued me from approaching destruction, I could have wished— honoring and respecting you as I had done your late friend— my excellent father—that you could have accepted a daughter's service from me. I do not pretend entirely to have surmounted these sentiments, although I have combated them, as being unworthy of me, and ungrateful to you. But, from the moment you were pleased to honor me by a claim on this poor hand, I have studiously examined my sentiments towards you, and taught myself so far to make them coincide with my duty, that I may call myself assured that De Lacy would not find in Eveline Berenger an indifferent, far less an unworthy bride. In this, sir, you may boldly confide, whether the union you have sought for takes place instantly, or is delayed till a longer season. Still farther, I must acknowledge that the postponement

of these nuptials will be more agreeable to me than their immediate accomplishment.   I am at present very young, and totally
inexperienced.   Two or three years will, I trust, render me yet
more worthy the regard of a man of honor."

At this declaration in his favor, however cold and qualified,
De Lacy had as much difficulty to restrain his transports as
formerly to moderate his agitation.

QUEEN BERENGARIA.

THE high-born Berengaria, daughter of Sanchez, King of
Navarre, and the Queen-Consort of the heroic Richard, was accounted one of the most beautiful women of the period. Her
form was slight, though exquisitely moulded. She was graced
with a complexion not common in her country, a profusion of
fair hair, and features so extremely juvenile, as to make her look
several years younger than she really was, though in reality she
was not above one-and-twenty. Perhaps it was under the consciousness of this extremely juvenile appearance, that she affected,
or at least practised, a little childish petulance, and wilfulness
of manner, not unbefitting, she might suppose, a youthful bride,
whose rank and age gave her a right to have her fantasies indulged and attended to. She was by nature perfectly good-
humored, and if her due share of admiration and homage (in her
opinion a very large one) was duly resigned to her, no one could
possess better temper, or a more friendly disposition ; but then,
like all despots, the more power that was voluntarily yielded to
her, the more she desired to extend her sway. Sometimes,
even when all her ambition was gratified, she chose to be a
little out of health, and a little out of spirits ; and physicians

had to toil their wits to invent names for imaginary maladies, while her ladies racked their imagination for new games, new head-gear, and new court-scandal, to pass away those unpleasant hours, during which their own situation was scarce to be greatly envied. Their most frequent resource for diverting this malady, was some trick, or piece of mischief, practised upon each other; and the good queen, in the buoyancy of her reviving spirits, was, to speak truth, rather too indifferent whether the frolics thus practised were entirely befitting her own dignity, or whether the pain which those suffered upon whom they were inflicted, was not beyond the proportion of pleasure which she herself derived from them. She was confident in her husband's favor, in her high rank, and in her supposed power to make good whatever such pranks might cost others. In a word, she gambolled with the freedom of a young lioness, who is unconscious of the weight of her own paws when laid on those whom she sports with.

The monarch was lying on his couch, and at some distance, as awaiting his farther commands, stood a man whose profession it was not difficult to conjecture. He was clothed in a jerkin of red cloth, which reached scantly below the shoulders, leaving the arms bare from about half-way above the elbow, and, as an upper garment, he wore, when about as at present to betake himself to his dreadful office, a coat or tabard without sleeves, something like that of a herald, made of dressed bull's hide, and stained in the front with many a broad spot and speckle of dull crimson. A cap of rough shag served to hide the upper part of a visage, which, like that of a screech-owl, seemed desirous to conceal itself from light—the lower part of the face being obscured by a huge red beard, mingling with shaggy locks of the same color. This official leant on a sword, the blade of which was nearly four feet and a half in length, while the handle of twenty inches, surrounded by a ring of lead plummets to counterpoise the weight of such a blade, rose considerably above the man's head, as he rested his arm upon its hilt, waiting for King Richard's farther directions.

On the sudden entrance of the ladies, Richard, who was then lying on his couch, with his face towards the entrance, and resting on his elbow as he spoke to his grisly attendant, flung himself hastily, as if displeased and surprised, to the other side, turning his back to the queen and the females of her train, and drawing around him the covering of his couch, which, by his own choice, or more probably the flattering selection of his chamberlains, consisted of two large lions' skins, dressed in Venice with such admirable skill, that they seemed softer than the hide of the deer.

Berengaria knew well—what woman knows not?—her own road to victory. After a hurried glance of undisguised and unaffected terror at the ghastly companion of her husband's secret councils, she rushed at once to the side of Richard's couch, dropped on her knees, flung her mantle from her shoulder, showing, as they hung down at their full length, her beautiful golden tresses, and while her countenance seemed like the sun bursting through a cloud, yet bearing on its pallid front traces that its splendors have been obscured, she seized upon the right hand of the king, which, as he assumed his wonted posture, had been employed in dragging the covering of his couch, and gradually pulling it to her with a force which was resisted, though but faintly, she possessed herself of that arm, the prop of Christendom, and the dread of Heathenesse, and imprisoning its strength in both her little fairy hands, she bent upon it her brow, and united to it her lips.

24

"What needs this, Berengaria?" said Richard, his head still averted, but his hand remaining under her control.

"Send away that man—his look kills me!" muttered Berengaria.

"Begone, sirrah," said Richard, still without looking round—"What wait'st thou for? art thou fit to look on these ladies?"

"Your Highness's pleasure touching the head," said the man.

"Out with thee, dog!" answered Richard—"a Christian burial."

The man disappeared, after casting a look upon the beautiful Queen, in her deranged dress and natural loveliness, with a smile of admiration more hideous in its expression than even his usual scowl of cynical hatred against humanity.

"And now, foolish wench, what wishest thou?" said Richard, turning slowly and half reluctantly round to his royal suppliant.

But it was not in nature for any one, far less an admirer of beauty like Richard, to whom it stood only in the second rank to glory, to look without emotion on the countenance and the tremor of a creature so beautiful as Berengaria, or to feel, without sympathy, that her lips, her brow, were on his hand, and that it was wetted by her tears. By degrees he turned on her his manly countenance, with the softest expression of which his large blue eye, which so often gleamed with insufferable light, was capable. Caressing her fair head, and mingling his large fingers in her beautiful and dishevelled locks, he raised and tenderly kissed the cherub countenance which seemed desirous to hide itself in his hand. The robust form, the broad, noble brow, and majestic looks, the naked arm and shoulder, the lions' skins among which he lay, and the fair, fragile, feminine creature that kneeled by his side, might have served for a model of Hercules reconciling himself, after a quarrel, to his wife Dejanira.

"And, once more, what seeks the lady of my heart in her knight's pavilion, at this unwonted hour?"

"Pardon, my most gracious liege, pardon!" said the Queen, whose fears began again to unfit her for the duty of intercessor.

"Pardon! for what?" asked the King.

"First, for entering your royal presence too boldly and unadvisedly"—

She stopped.

"*Thou* too boldly!—the sun might as well ask pardon because his rays entered the windows of some wretch's dungeon. But I was busied with work unfit for thee to witness, my gentle one, and I was unwilling, besides, that thou shouldst risk thy precious health where sickness has been so lately rife."

"But thou art now well?" said the Queen, still delaying the communication which she feared to make.

"Well enough to break a lance on the bold crest of that champion who shall refuse to acknowledge thee the fairest dame in Christendom."

"Thou wilt not then refuse me one boon—only one—only a poor life?"

"Ha!—proceed," said Richard, bending his brows.

"This unhappy Scottish knight," murmured the Queen.

"Speak not of him, madam," exclaimed Richard, sternly; "he dies—his doom is fixed."

"Nay, my royal liege and love, 'tis but a silken banner neglected.—Berengaria will give thee another, broidered with her own hand, and rich as ever dallied with the wind. Every pearl I have shall go to bedeck it, and with every pearl I will drop a tear of thankfulness to my generous knight!"

"Away, away," cried the King, "the sun has risen on the dishonor of England, and it is not yet avenged. Withdraw, if ye would not hear orders which would displease you; for, by St. George, I swear"—

"Swear NOT!" said the voice of one who had just then entered the pavilion.

"Ha! my learned Hakim," said the King; "come, I hope, to tax our generosity."

"I come to request instant speech with you—instant—and touching matters of deep interest."

"First look on my wife, Hakim, and let her know in you the preserver of her husband."

"It is not for me," said the physician, bending his eyes on the ground—"it is not for me to look upon beauty unveiled, and armed in its splendors."

"Retire, then, Berengaria," said the monarch; "and Edith, do you retire also;—nay, renew not your importunities! This I give to them, that the execution shall not be till high noon. Go and be pacified—dearest Berengaria, begone."

ALICE LEE.

"Ah! Alice Lee—so sweet, so gentle, so condescending in thy loveliness—[thus proceeds a contemporary annalist, whose manuscript we have deciphered]—why is my story to turn upon thy fallen fortunes? and why not rather to the period when, in the very dismounting from your palfrey, you attracted as many eyes as if an angel had descended,—as many blessings as if the benignant being had come fraught with good tidings? No creature wert thou of an idle romancer's imagination—no being fantastically bedizened with inconsistent perfections;—thy merits made me love thee well—and for thy faults—so well did they show amid thy good qualities, that I think they made me love thee better."

Sir Henry Lee sat in a wicker arm-chair by the fire. He was wrapped in a cloak, and his limbs extended on a stool, as if he were suffering from gout or indisposition. His long white beard flowing over the dark-colored garment, gave him more the appearance of a hermit than of an aged soldier or man of quality; and that character was increased by the deep and devout attention with which he listened to a respectable old man, whose dilapidated dress showed still something of the clerical habit, and who, with a low, but full and deep voice, was reading the Evening Service according to the Church of England. Alice Lee kneeled at the feet of her father, and made the responses with a voice that might have suited the choir of angels, and a modest and serious devotion, which suited the melody of her tone.

When Colonel Everard entered, the clergyman raised his finger, as cautioning him to forbear disturbing the divine service of the evening, and pointed to a seat; to which, struck deeply with the scene he had witnessed, the intruder stole with as light a step as possible, and knelt devoutly down as one of the little congregation.

Everard had been bred by his father what was called a Puritan ; a member of a sect who, in the primitive sense of the word, were persons that did not except against the doctrines of the Church of England, or even in all respects against its hierarchy.

Yet deep as was the habitual veneration with which he heard the impressive service of the Church, Everard's eyes could not help straying towards Alice, and his thoughts wandering to the purpose of his presence there.   She seemed to have recognized him at once, for there was a deeper glow than usual upon her cheek, her fingers trembled as they turned the leaves of her prayer-book, and her voice, lately as firm as it was melodious, faltered when she repeated the responses.   It appeared to Everard, as far as he could collect by the stolen glances which he directed towards her, that the character of her beauty, as well as of her outward appearance, had changed with her fortunes.

The beautiful and high-born young lady had now approached as nearly as possible to the brown stuff dress of an ordinary village maiden ; but what she had lost in gayety of appearance, she had gained as it seemed in dignity. Her beautiful light-brown tresses, now folded around her head, and only curled where nature had so arranged them, gave her an air of simplicity, which did not exist when her head-dress showed the skill of a curious tire-woman. A light joyous air, with something of a humorous expression, which seemed to be looking for amusement, had vanished before the touch of affliction, and a calm melancholy supplied its place, which seemed on the watch to administer comfort to others. Perhaps the former arch, though innocent expression of countenance, was uppermost in her lover's recollection, when he concluded that Alice had acted a part in the disturbances which had taken place at the Lodge. It is certain, that when he now looked upon her, it was with shame for having nourished such a suspicion, and the resolution to believe rather that the devil had imitated her voice, than that a creature, who seemed so much above the feelings of this world, and so nearly allied to the purity of the next, should have had the indelicacy to mingle in such manœuvres as he himself and others had been subjected to.

These thoughts shot through his mind, in spite of the impropriety of indulging them at such a moment. The service now approached the close ; and a good deal to Colonel Everard's surprise as well as confusion, the officiating priest, in firm and audible tone, and with every attribute of dignity, prayed to the Almighty to bless and preserve " Our Sovereign Lord, King Charles, the lawful and undoubted King of these realms." The petition (in those days most dangerous) was pronounced with a full, raised, and distinct articulation, as if the priest challenged all who heard him to dissent if they dared. If the republican officer did not assent to the petition, he thought at least it was no time to protest against it.

The service was concluded in the usual manner, and Colonel Everard, approaching his uncle's seat, made a deep inclination of respect, first to Sir Henry Lee, and then to Alice, whose color now spread from her cheek to her brow and bosom.

"I have to crave your excuse," said the Colonel with hesitation, "for having chosen for my visit, which I dare not hope would be very agreeable at any time, a season most peculiarly unsuitable."

"So far from it, nephew," answered Sir Henry, with much more mildness of manner than Everard had dared to expect, "that your visits at other times would be much more welcome, had we the fortune to see you often at our hours of worship. But it was, I ween, not to settle jarring creeds, that you have honored our poor dwelling, where, to say the truth, we dared scarce have expected to see you again, so coarse was our last welcome."

"I should be happy to believe," said Colonel Everard, hesitating, "that—that—in short my presence was not now so unwelcome here as on that occasion."

"Nephew," said Sir Henry, "I will be frank with you. When you were last here, I thought you had stolen from me a precious pearl, which at one time it would have been my pride and happiness to have bestowed on you; but which, being such as you have been of late, I would bury in the depths of the earth rather than give to your keeping. This somewhat chafed, as honest Will says, 'the rash humor which my mother gave me.' I thought I was robbed, and I thought I saw the robber before me. I am mistaken.—I am not robbed; and the attempt without the deed I can pardon."

"I would not willingly seek offence in your words, sir," said Colonel Everard, "when their general purport sounds kind;

but I can protest before Heaven, that my views and wishes towards you and your family are as void of selfish hopes and selfish ends, as they are fraught with love to you and to yours."

"Sir, if I retract my opinion, which is not my wont, you shall hear of it.—And now, cousin, have you more to say? We keep that worthy clergyman in the outer room."

"Something I had to say—something touching my cousin Alice," said Everard, with embarrassment; "but I fear that the prejudices of both are so strong against me "——

"Sir, I dare turn my daughter loose to you—I will go join the good doctor in dame Joan's apartment. I am not unwilling that you should know that the girl hath, in all reasonable sort, the exercise of her free will."

He withdrew and left the cousins together.

Colonel Everard advanced to Alice, and was about to take her hand. She drew back, took the seat which her father had occupied, and pointed out to him one at some distance.

"Are we then so much estranged, my dearest Alice?" he said.

"We will speak of that presently," she replied. "In the first place, let me ask the cause of your visit here at so late an hour."

"You heard," said Everard, "what I stated to your father?"

"I did; but that seems to have been only part of your errand—something there seemed to be which applied particularly to me."

"It was a fancy—a strange mistake," answered Everard. "May I ask if you have been abroad this evening?"

"Certainly not," she replied. "I have small temptation to wander from my present home, poor as it is; and whilst here, I have important duties to discharge. But why does Colonel Everard ask so strange a question?"

25

"Tell me in turn, why your cousin Markham has lost the name of friendship and kindred, and even of some nearer feeling, and then I will answer you, Alice."

"It is soon answered," she said. "When you drew your sword against my father's cause—almost against his person—I studied, more than I should have done, to find excuse for you. I knew, that is, I thought I knew, your high feelings of public duty—I knew the opinions in which you had been bred up; and I said, I will not even for this cast him off—he opposes his King because he is loyal to his country. You endeavored to avert the great and concluding tragedy of the 30th of January; and it confirmed me in my opinion, that Markham Everard might been misled, but could not be base or selfish."

"And what has changed your opinion, Alice? or who dare," said Everard, reddening, "attach such epithets to the name of Markham Everard?"

"I am no subject," she said, "for exercising your valor, Colonel Everard, nor do I mean to offend. But you will find enough of others who will avow, that Colonel Everard is truckling to the usurper Cromwell, and that all his fair pretexts of forwarding his country's liberties are but a screen for driving a bargain with the successful encroacher, and obtaining the best terms he can for himself and his family."

"For myself?—Never!"

"But for your family you have.—Yes, I am well assured that you have pointed out to the military tyrant the way in which he and his satraps may master the government. Do you think my father or I would accept an asylum purchased at the price of England's liberty, and your honor?"

"Gracious Heaven, Alice, what is this? You accuse me of pursuing the very course which so lately had your approbation!"

"When you spoke with authority of your father, and recommended our submission to the existing government, such as it was, I own I thought that my father's gray head might, without dishonor, have remained under the roof where it had so long been sheltered. But did your father sanction your becoming the adviser of yonder ambitious soldier to a new course of innovation, and his abettor in the establishment of a new species of tyranny?—It is one thing to submit to oppression, another to be the agent of tyrants.—And oh, Markham—their bloodhound!"

"How! bloodhound?—what mean you?—I own it is true I could see with content the wounds of this bleeding country stanched, even at the expense of beholding Cromwell, after his matchless rise, take a yet further step to power—but to be his bloodhound! What is your meaning?"

"It is false, then?—Ah, I thought I could swear it had been false?"

"What, in the name of God, is it you ask?"

"It is false that you are engaged to betray the young King of Scotland?"

"Betray him! *I* betray him, or any fugitive? Never! I would he were well out of England—I would lend him my aid to escape, were he in the house at this instant; and think in acting so I did his enemies good service, by preventing their soiling themselves with his blood—but betray him, never!"

"I knew it—I was sure it was impossible. Oh, be yet more honest; disengage yourself from yonder gloomy and ambitious soldier! Shun him and his schemes, which are formed in injustice, and can only be realized in yet more blood!"

"Believe me," replied Everard, "that I choose the line of policy best befitting the times."

"Choose that," she said, "which best befits duty, Markham —which best befits truth and honor. Do your duty, and let Providence decide the rest.—Farewell! we tempt my father's patience too far—you know his temper—farewell, Markham."

She extended her hand, which he pressed to his lips, and left the apartment.

THE GLEE-MAIDEN.

Fair is the damsel, passing fair—
Sunny at distance gleams her smile :
Approach—the cloud of woeful care
Hangs trembling in her eye the while.

LUCINDA, *a Ballad*.

THE glee-maiden had planted herself where a rise of two
large broad steps, giving access to the main gateway of the
royal apartments, gained her an advantage of a foot and a half
in height over those in the court, of whom she hoped to form an
audience. She wore the dress of her calling, which was more
gaudy than rich, and showed the person more than did the
garb of other females. She had laid aside an upper mantle,
and a small basket which contained her slender stock of neces-
saries, and a little French spaniel dog sat beside them, as their
protector. An azure-blue jacket, embroidered with silver, and
sitting close to the person, was open in front, and showed several
waistcoats of different-colored silks, calculated to set off the
symmetry of the shoulders and bosom, and remaining open at
the throat. A small silver chain worn around her neck, involved
itself amongst these brilliant-colored waistcoats, and was again
produced from them, to display a medal of the same metal,

which intimated, in the name of some court or guild of minstrels, the degree she had taken in the Gay or Joyous Science.
A small scrip, suspended over her shoulders by a blue silk ribbon,
hung on her left side.

Her sunny complexion, snow-white teeth, brilliant black
eyes, and raven locks, marked her country lying far in the south
of France, and the arch smile and dimpled chin bore the same
character. Her luxuriant raven locks, twisted around a small
gold bodkin, were kept in their position by a net of silk and
gold. Short petticoats, deep-laced with silver, to correspond
with the jacket, red stockings which were visible so high as
near the calf of the leg, and buskins of Spanish leather, com-
pleted her adjustment, which, though far from new, had been
saved as an untarnished holiday suit, which much care had kept
in good order. She seemed about twenty-five years old ; but
perhaps fatigue and wandering had anticipated the touch of time,
in obliterating the freshness of early youth.

We have said the glee-maiden's manner was lively, and we
may add, that her smile and repartee were ready. But her
gayety was assumed, as a quality essentially necessary to her
trade, of which it was one of the miseries, that the professors
were obliged frequently to cover an aching heart with a compelled smile. This seemed to be the case with Louise, who,
whether she was really the heroine of her own song, or whatever
other cause she might have for sadness, showed at times a strain
of deep melancholy thought, which interfered with and con-
trolled the natural flow of lively spirits, which the practice of
the Joyous Science especially required. She lacked also, even
in her gayest sallies, the decided boldness and effrontery of her
sisterhood, who were seldom at a loss to retort a saucy jest, or turn
the laugh against any who interrupted or interfered with them.

It may be here remarked, that it was impossible that this class of women, very numerous in that age, could bear a character generally respectable. They were, however, protected by the manners of the time; and such were the immunities they possessed by the rights of chivalry, that nothing was more rare than to hear of such errant damsels sustaining injury or wrong, and they passed and repassed safely, where armed travellers would probably have encountered a bloody opposition. But though licensed and protected in honor of their tuneful art, the wandering minstrels, male or female, like similar ministers to the public amusement, the itinerant musicians, for instance, and strolling comedians of our own day, led a life too irregular and precarious, to be accounted a creditable part of society. Indeed, among the stricter Catholics, the profession was considered as unlawful.

Such was the damsel, who, with viol in hand, and stationed on the slight elevation we have mentioned, stepped forward to the bystanders and announced herself as a mistress of the Gay Science, duly qualified by a brief from a Court of Love and Music held at Aix, in Provence, under the countenance of the flower of chivalry, the gallant Count Aymer; who now prayed that the cavaliers of merry Scotland, who were known over the wide world for bravery and courtesy, would permit a poor stranger to try whether she could afford them any amusement by her art.—The love of song was, like the love of fight, a common passion of the age, which all at least affected, whether they were actually possessed by it or no; therefore the acquiescence in Louise's proposal was universal. At the same time, an aged, dark-browed monk, who was among the bystanders, thought it necessary to remind the glee-maiden, that, since she was tolerated within these precincts, which was an unusual grace, he trusted nothing would be sung or said inconsistent with the holy character of the place.

The glee-maiden bent her head low, shook her sable locks, and crossed herself reverentially, as if she disclaimed the possibility of such a transgression, and then began the song. The tune, which was played upon a viol, was gay and sprightly in the commencement, with a touch of the wildness of the Troubadour music. But as it proceeded, the faltering tones of the instrument, and of the female voice which accompanied it, became plaintive and interrupted, as if choked by the painful feelings of the minstrel. The song was in the Provençal dialect, well understood as the language of poetry in all the courts of Europe, and particularly in Scotland. It was more simply turned, however, than was the general caste of the Sirventes, and rather resembled the *lai* of a Norman Minstrel. It may be translated thus :

THE LAY OF POOR LOUISE.

Ah, poor Louise ! The livelong day
She roams from cot to castle gay ;
And still her voice and viol say,
Ah, maids, beware the woodland way,
                    Think on Louise.

Ah, poor Louise ! The sun was high,
It smirch'd her cheek, it dimm'd her eye,
The woodland walk was cool and nigh,
Where birds with chiming streamlets vie
                    To cheer Louise.

Ah, poor Louise ! The savage bear
Made ne'er that lovely grove his lair;
The wolves molest not paths so fair—
But better far had such been there
                    For poor Louise.

Ah, poor Louise! In woody wold
She met a huntsman fair and bold;
His baldrick was of silk and gold,
And many a witching tale he told
                    To poor Louise.

Ah, poor Louise! Small cause to pine
Hadst thou for treasures of the mine;
For peace of mind, that gift divine,
And spotless innocence, were thine,
                    Ah, poor Louise.

Ah, poor Louise! Thy treasure's reft!
I know not if by force or theft,
Or part by violence, part by gift;
But misery is all that's left
                    To poor Louise.

Let poor Louise some succor have!
She will not long your bounty crave,
Or tire the gay with warning stave—
For Heaven has grace, and earth a grave
                    For poor Louise.

Just as she commenced, was heard a cry of " Room—room—
place for the Duke of Rothsay ! "

" Nay, hurry no man on my score," said a gallant young
cavalier, who entered on a noble Arabian horse, which he
managed with exquisite grace, though by such slight handling
of the reins, such imperceptible pressure of the limbs and sway
of the body, that to any eye save that of an experienced horse-
man, the animal seemed to be putting forth his paces for his
own amusement, and thus gracefully bearing forward a rider
who was too indolent to give himself any trouble about the
matter.

The Prince's apparel, which was very rich, was put on with
26

slovenly carelessness. His form, though his stature was low, and his limbs extremely slight, was elegant in the extreme ; and his features no less handsome. But there was on his brow a haggard paleness, which seemed the effect of care or of dissipation, or of both these wasting causes combined. His eyes were sunk and dim, as from late indulgence in revelry on the preceding evening, while his cheek was inflamed with unnatural red, as if either the effect of the Bacchanalian orgies had not passed away from the constitution, or a morning draught had been resorted to, in order to remove the effects of the night's debauchery.

Such was the Duke of Rothsay, and heir of the Scottish crown, a sight at once of interest and compassion. All unbonneted, and made way for him, while he kept repeating carelessly, " No haste—no haste.—I shall arrive soon enough at the place I am bound for.—How's this—a damsel of the Joyous Science ? Ay, by St. Giles ! and a comely wench to boot. Stand still, my merry men ; never was minstrelsy marred for me.—A good voice, by the mass ! Begin me that lay again, sweetheart."

Louise did not know the person who addressed her ; but the general respect paid by all around, and the easy and indifferent manner in which it was received, showed her she was addressed by a man of the highest quality. She recommenced her lay, and sung her best accordingly ; while the young Duke seemed thoughtful and rather affected towards the close of the ditty. But it was not his habit to cherish such melancholy affections. " This is a plaintive ditty, my nut-brown maid," said he, chucking the retreating glee-maiden under the chin, and detaining her by the collar of her dress, which was not difficult, as he sat on horseback so close to the steps on which she stood.   " But I warrant me you have livelier notes at will, *ma bella tenebrosa ;* ay, and canst sing in bower as well as wold, and by night as well as day."

" I am no nightingale, my lord," said Louise, endeavoring to escape a species of gallantry which ill-suited the place and circumstances, a discrepancy to which he who addressed it to her seemed contemptuously indifferent.

" What hast thou there, darling ? " he added, removing his hold from her collar, to the scrip which she carried.

Glad was Louise to escape his grasp, by slipping the knot of her ribbon, and leaving the little bag in the Prince's hand, as, retiring back, beyond his reach, she answered, " Nuts, my lord, of the last season."

The Prince pulled out a handful of nuts accordingly. " Nuts, child !—they will break thine ivory teeth—hurt thy pretty voice," said Rothsay, cracking one with his teeth, like a village schoolboy.

" They are not the walnuts of my own sunny clime, my lord," said Louise ; " but they hang low, and are within the reach of the poor."

" You shall have something to afford you better fare, poor wandering ape," said the Duke, in a tone in which feeling predominated more than in the affected and contemptuous gallantry of his first address to the glee-maiden.

At this moment, as he turned to ask an attendant for his purse, the Prince encountered the stern and piercing look of a tall black man, seated on a powerful iron-gray horse, who had entered the court with attendants while the Duke of Rothsay was engaged with Louise, and now remained stupefied and almost turned to stone by his surprise and anger at this unseemly spectacle. Even one who had never seen Archibald, Earl

of Douglas, called the Grim, must have known him by his swart
complexion, his gigantic frame, his buff-coat of bull's hide, and
his air of courage, firmness, and sagacity, mixed with indomitable
pride. The loss of an eye in battle, though not perceptible at
first sight, as the ball of the injured organ remained similar to
the other, gave yet a stern immovable glare to the whole aspect.

The meeting of the royal son-in-law with his terrible step-
father, was in circumstances which arrested the attention of all
present; and the bystanders waited the issue with silence and
suppressed breath, lest they should lose any part of what was
to ensue.

When the Duke of Rothsay saw the expression which occupied the stern features of Douglas, and remarked that the
Earl did not make the least motion towards respectful, or even
civil salutation, he seemed determined to show him how little respect he was disposed to pay to his displeased looks. He took
his purse from his chamberlain.

"Here, pretty one," he said, "I give thee one gold piece
for the song thou hast sung me, another for the nuts I have
stolen from thee, and a third for the kiss thou art about to give
me. For know, my pretty one, that when fair lips (and thine,
for fault of better, may be called so) make sweet music for my
pleasure, I am sworn to St. Valentine to press them to mine."

"My song is recompensed nobly"—said Louise, shrinking
back; "my nuts are sold to a good market—farther traffic, my
lord, were neither befitting you nor beseeming me."

"What! you coy it, my nymph of the highway?" said the
Prince, contemptuously. "Know, damsel, that one asks you
a grace who is unused to denial."

"It is the Prince of Scotland"—"the Duke of Rothsay,"—
said the courtiers around, to the terrified Louise, pressing for-

ward the trembling young woman; "you must not thwart his humor."

"But I cannot reach your lordship," she said timidly, "you sit so high on horseback."

"If I must alight," said Rothsay, "there shall be the heavier penalty—What does the wench tremble for? Place thy foot on the toe of my boot, give me hold of thy hand—Gallantly done!" He kissed her as she stood thus suspended in the air, perched upon his foot, and supported by his hand; saying, "There is thy kiss, and there is my purse to pay it; and to grace thee farther, Rothsay will wear the scrip for the day." He suffered the frightened girl to spring to the ground, and turned his looks from her to bend them contemptuously on the Earl of Douglas, as if he had said, "All this I do in despite of you and of your daughter's claims."

"By St. Bride of Douglas!" said the Earl, pressing towards the Prince, "this is too much, unmannered boy, as void of sense as honor! You know what considerations restrain the hand of Douglas, else had you never dared "——

"Can you play at spang-cockle, my lord?" said the Prince, placing a nut on the second joint of his forefinger, and spinning it off by a smart application of the thumb. The nut struck on Douglas's broad breast, who burst out into a dreadful exclamation of wrath, inarticulate, but resembling the growl of a lion in depth and sternness of expression. "I cry your pardon, most mighty lord," said the Duke of Rothsay, scornfully, while all around trembled; "I did not conceive my pellet could have wounded you, seeing you wear a buff-coat. Surely, I trust, it did not hit your eye?"

The Prior, despatched by the King, as we have seen in the last chapter, had by this time made way through the crowd, and

laying hold on Douglas's rein, in a manner that made it impossible for him to advance, reminded him that the Prince was the
son of his Sovereign, and the husband of his daughter.

"Fear not, Sir Prior," said Douglas. "I despise the childish
boy too much to raise a finger against him. But I will return
insult for insult.—Here, any of you who love the Douglas,—
spurn me this quean from the Monastery gates; and let her be
so scourged that she may bitterly remember to the last day of
her life, how she gave means to an unrespective boy to affront
the Douglas!"

Four or five retainers instantly stepped forth to execute commands which were seldom uttered in vain, and heavily would
Louise have atoned for an offence of which she was alike the innocent, unconscious, and unwilling instrument, had not the Duke
of Rothsay interfered.

"Spurn the poor glee-woman!" he said in high indignation;
"scourge her for obeying my commands!—Spurn thine own
oppressed vassals, rude Earl—scourge thine own faulty hounds
—but beware how you touch so much as a dog that Rothsay hath
patted on the head, far less a female whose lips he hath kissed!"

"By St. Bride of Douglas, I will be avenged!" said the
Earl. "No man shall brook life after he has passed an affront
on Douglas."

"Why so you may be avenged in fitting time," said Albany;
"but let it not be said, that, like a peevish woman, the Great
Douglas could choose neither time nor place for his vengeance."

George of March, in the meanwhile, had a more easy task
of pacifying the Prince. "My Lord of Rothsay," he said,
approaching him with grave ceremony, "I need not tell you that
you owe me something for reparation of honor, though I blame
not you personally for the breach of contract which has destroyed

the peace of my family. Let me conjure you by what observance your Highness may owe an injured man, to forego for the
present this scandalous dispute."

"My lord, I owe you much," replied Rothsay; "but this
haughty and all-controlling lord has wounded mine honor."

"My lord, I can but add, your royal father is ill—hath
swooned with terror for your Highness's safety."

"Ill!" replied the Prince; "the kind, good old man—
swooned, said you, my Lord of March?—I am with him in an
instant."

The Duke of Rothsay sprung from his saddle to the ground,
and was dashing into the palace like a greyhound, when a feeble
grasp was laid on his cloak, and the faint voice of a kneeling
female exclaimed, "Protection, my noble Prince!—Protection
for a helpless stranger!"

"Hands off, stroller!" said the Earl of March, thrusting
the suppliant glee-maiden aside.

But the gentler Prince paused. "It is true," he said, "I
have brought the vengeance of an unforgiving devil upon this
helpless creature. O Heaven! what a life is mine, so fatal to
all who approach me!—What to do in the hurry?—She must
not go to my apartments—And all my men are such born rep-
robates.—Ha! thou at mine elbow, honest Harry Smith?
What dost thou here?"

"There has been something of a fight, my lord," answered
our acquaintance the Smith, "between the townsmen and the
Southland loons who ride with the Douglas; and we have
swinged them as far as the Abbey-Gate."

"I am glad of it—I am glad of it. And you beat the
knaves fairly?"

"Fairly, does your Highness ask?" said Henry. "Why,

ay! We were stronger in numbers, to be sure; but no men ride better armed than those who follow the Bloody Heart. And so in a sense we beat them fairly; for as your Highness knows, it is the Smith who makes the man-at-arms, and men with good weapons are a match for great odds."

"I had something to say to thee, Smith—Canst thou take up a fallen link in my Milan hauberk?"

"As well, please your Highness, as my mother could take up a stitch in the nets she wove—The Milaner shall not know my work from his own."

"Well, but that was not what I wished of thee just now," said the Prince, recollecting himself; "this poor glee-woman, good Smith, she must be placed in safety. Thou art man enough to be any woman's champion, and thou must conduct her to some place of safety."

Henry Smith was, as we have seen, sufficiently rash and daring when weapons were in question. But he had also the pride of a decent burgher, and was unwilling to place himself in what might be thought equivocal circumstances by the sober part of his fellow-citizens.

"May it please your Highness," he said, "I am but a poor craftsman. But though my arm and sword are at the King's service, and your Highness's, I am, with reverence, no squire of dames. Your Highness will find, among your own retinue, knights and lords willing enough to play Sir Pandarus of Troy —it is too knightly a part for poor Hal of the Wynd."

"Umph—hah!" said the Prince. "My purse, Edgar,"— (his attendant whispered him)—"True, true, I gave it to the poor wench. I know enough of your craft, Sir Smith, and of craftsmen in general, to be aware that men lure not hawks with empty hands; but I suppose my word may pass for the price of a good armor, and I will pay it thee with thanks to boot for this slight service."

"Your Highness may know other craftsmen," said the Smith; "but, with reverence, you know not Henry Gow. He will obey you in making a weapon, or in wielding one, but he knows nothing of this petticoat service."

"Hark thee, thou Perthshire mule," said the Prince, yet smiling, while he spoke, at the sturdy punctilio of the honest burgher—"the wench is as little to me as she is to thee. But in an idle moment, as you may learn from those about thee, if thou sawest it not thyself, I did her a passing grace, which is likely to cost the poor wretch her life. There is no one here whom I can trust to protect her against the discipline of belt and bowstring, with which the Border brutes who follow Douglas will beat her to death, since such is his pleasure."

"If such be the case, my liege, she has a right to every honest man's protection; and since she wears a petticoat— though I would it were longer, and of a less fanciful fashion—I will answer for her protection as well as a single man may."

Then, as if afraid of farther objection on the Smith's part, the Prince hastened into the palace.

Henry Gow remained stupefied at what had passed, and at finding himself involved in a charge at once inferring much danger, and an equal risk of scandal, both which, joined to a principal share which he had taken, with his usual forwardness, in the fray, might, he saw, do him no small injury in the suit he pursued most anxiously. At the same time, to leave a defenceless creature to the ill-usage of the barbarous Galwegians, and licentious followers of the Douglas, was a thought which his manly heart could not brook for an instant.

The Smith put himself in motion, with a sigh much resem-

27

bling a groan, and took his way through a postern door, which, after looking once behind him, he left ajar. Behind him followed Louise, who had hastily assumed her small bundle, and, calling her little four-legged companion, had eagerly followed in the path which opened an escape from what had shortly before seemed a great and inevitable danger.

CATHERINE THE FAIR MAID OF PERTH.

The glee-woman had been abroad upon the sixth day, a little before noon; and the desire of fresh air, or the hope to find some salad or potherbs, or at least an early flower or two, with which to deck their board, had carried her into the small garden appertaining to the castle. She re-entered her apartment in the tower with a countenance pale as ashes, and a frame which trembled like an aspen leaf. Her terror instantly extended itself to Catherine, who could hardly find words to ask what new misfortune had occurred.

"Is the Duke of Rothsay dead?"

"Worse! they are starving him alive."

"Madness, woman!"

"No, no, no, no!" said Louise, speaking under her breath, and huddling her words so thick upon each other, that Catherine could hardly catch the sense. "I was seeking for flowers to dress your pottage, because you said you loved them yesterday—my poor little dog, thrusting himself into a thicket of yew and holly bushes that grow out of some old ruins close to the castle wall, came back whining and howling. I crept forward to see what might be the cause—and, oh! I heard a groaning as of one in extreme pain, but so faint, that it seemed to arise out of the very depth of the earth. At length, I found it proceeded from a small rent in the wall, covered with ivy; and when I laid my ear close to the opening, I could hear the Prince's voice distinctly say, 'It cannot now last long;' and then it sunk away in something like a prayer."

"Gracious Heaven! did you speak to him?"

"I said, 'Is it you, my lord?' and the answer was, 'Who mocks me with that title?' I asked him if I could help him, and he answered with a voice I shall never forget, 'Food! food! I die of famine!' So I came hither to tell you. What is to be done?"

"I know not yet," said Catherine, prompt and bold on occasions of moment, though yielding to her companion in ingenuity of resource on ordinary occasions. "I know not yet— but something we will do—the blood of Bruce shall not die unaided."

So saying, she seized the small cruse which contained their soup, and the meat of which it was made, wrapped some thin cakes which she had baked, into the fold of her plaid, and, beckoning her companion to follow with a vessel of milk, also part of their provisions, she hastened towards the garden.

Louise indicated to her a heap of ruins, which, covered with underwood, was close to the castle wall. It had probably been originally a projection from the building; and the small fissure, which communicated with the dungeon, contrived for air, had terminated within it. But the aperture had been a little enlarged by decay, and admitted a dim ray of light to its recesses, although it could not be observed by those who visited the place with torchlight aids.

"Here is dead silence," said Catherine, after she had

listened attentively for a moment. "Heaven and earth, he is gone!"

"We must risk something," said her companion, and ran her fingers over the strings of her guitar.

A sigh was the only answer from the depth of the dungeon. Catherine then ventured to speak. "I am here, my lord—I am here, with food and drink."

"Ha! Ramorny? The jest comes too late—I am dying," was the answer.

"His brain is turned, and no wonder," thought Catherine. "It is I, my lord, Catherine Glover. I have food, if I could pass it safely to you."

"Heaven bless thee, maiden! I thought the pain was over, but it glows again within me at the name of food."

"The food is here, but how, ah how can I pass it to you? the chink is so narrow, the wall is so thick. Yet there is a remedy—I have it. Quick, Louise; cut me a willow bough, the tallest you can find."

The glee-maiden obeyed, and by means of a cleft in the top of the wand, Catherine transmitted several morsels of the soft cakes, soaked in broth, which served at once for food and for drink.

The unfortunate young man ate little, and with difficulty, but prayed for a thousand blessings on the head of his comforter. "I had destined thee to be the slave of my vices," he said, "and yet thou triest to become the preserver of my life! But away, and save thyself!"

"I will return with food as I shall see opportunity," said Catherine, just as the glee-maiden plucked her sleeve, and desired her to be silent, and stand close.

Both couched among the ruins, and they heard the voices of Ramorny and the mediciner in close conversation.

"He is stronger than I thought," said the former, in a low, croaking tone. "Were it not better end the matter more speedily? The Black Douglas comes this way. He is not in Albany's secret. He will demand to see the Prince, and all *must* be over ere he comes."

They passed on in their dark and fatal conversation.

"Now gain we the tower," said Catherine to her companion, when she saw they had left the garden. "I had a plan of escape for myself—I will turn it into one of rescue for the Prince. The dey-woman enters the Castle about vesper time, and usually leaves her cloak in the passage as she goes into the pantler's office with the milk. Take thou the cloak, muffle thyself close, and pass the warder boldly; he is usually drunken at that hour, and thou wilt go, as the dey-woman, unchallenged through gate and along bridge, if thou bear thyself with confidence. Then away to meet the Black Douglas; he is our nearest and only aid. Tell him that his son-in-law, the Prince of Scotland, dies —treacherously famished—in Falkland Castle, and thou wilt merit not pardon only, but reward."

"I care not for reward," said Louise; "the deed will reward itself."

They sobbed in each other's arms, and the intervening hours till evening were spent in endeavoring to devise some better mode of supplying the captive with nourishment, and in the construction of a tube, composed of hollow reeds, slipping into each other, by which liquids might be conveyed to him. The bell of the village church of Falkland tolled to vespers. The dey, or farm-woman, entered with her pitchers, to deliver the milk for the family, and to hear and tell the news stirring. She had scarcely entered the kitchen, when the female minstrel, again throwing herself in Catherine's arms, and assuring her of her unalterable fidelity, crept in silence down stairs, the little dog under her arm. A moment after, she was seen by the breathless Catherine, wrapt in the dey-woman's cloak, and walking composedly across the drawbridge.

The hour of dinner alone afforded a space, when, all in the Castle being occupied with that meal, Catherine thought she had the best opportunity of venturing to the breach in the wall, with the least chance of being observed. In waiting for the hour, she observed some stir in the Castle, which had been silent as the grave ever since the seclusion of the Duke of Rothsay. The portcullis was lowered and raised, and the creaking of the machinery was intermingled with the tramp of horse, as men-at-arms went out and returned with steeds hard-ridden and covered with foam. She observed, too, that such domestics as she casually saw from her window were in arms. All this made her heart throb high, for it augured the approach of rescue ; and besides, the bustle left the little garden more lonely than ever. At length, the hour of noon arrived; she had taken care to provide, under pretence of her own wishes, which the pantler seemed disposed to indulge, such articles of food as could be the most easily conveyed to the unhappy captive. She whispered to intimate her presence—there was no answer—she spoke louder ; still there was silence.

" He sleeps "—she muttered these words half aloud, and with a shuddering which was succeeded by a start and a scream, when a voice replied behind her,—

" Yes, he sleeps; but it is for ever."

She looked round. Sir John Ramorny stood behind her in complete armor, but the visor of his helmet was up, and displayed a countenance more resembling one about to die than to fight. He spoke with a grave tone, something between that of a calm observer of an interesting event, and of one who is an agent and partaker in it.

"Catherine," he said, "all is true which I tell you. He is dead—you have done your best for him—you can do no more."

ANNE OF GEIERSTEIN.

ARTHUR PHILIPSON had commenced his precarious journey along the precipice, with all the coolness, resolution, and un- shaken determination of mind, which was most essential to a task where all must depend upon firmness of nerve. But the formidable accident which checked his onward progress was of a character so dreadful, as made him feel all the bitterness of a death, instant, horrible, and, as it seemed, inevitable. The solid rock had trembled and rent beneath his footsteps, and although, by an effort rather mechanical than voluntary, he had withdrawn himself from the instant ruin attending its descent, he felt as if the better part of him, his firmness of mind and strength of body, had been rent away with the descending rock, as it fell thundering, with clouds of dust and smoke, into the torrents and whirlpools of the vexed gulf beneath. In fact, the seaman swept from the deck of a wrecked vessel, drenched in the waves, and battered against the rocks on the shore, does not differ more from the same mariner, when, at the commencement of the gale, he stood upon the deck of his favorite ship, proud of her strength and his own dexterity, than Arthur, when commencing his jour- ney, from the same Arthur, while clinging to the decayed trunk

28

of an old tree, from which, suspended between heaven and earth, he saw the fall of the crag which he had so nearly accompanied.

An incident, in itself trifling, added to the distress occasioned by this alienation of his powers. All living things in the neighborhood had, as might be supposed, been startled by the tremendous fall to which his progress had given occasion. Flights of owls, bats, and other birds of darkness, compelled to betake themselves to the air, had lost no time in returning into their bowers of ivy, or the harbor afforded them by the rifts and holes of the neighboring rocks. One of this ill-omened flight chanced to be a lammer-geier, or Alpine vulture, a bird larger and more voracious than the eagle himself, and which Arthur had not been accustomed to see, or at least to look upon closely. With the instinct of most birds of prey, it is the custom of this creature, when gorged with food, to assume some station of inaccessible security, and there remain stationary and motionless for days together, till the work of digestion has been accomplished, and activity returns with the pressure of appetite. Disturbed from such a state of repose, one of these terrific birds had risen from the ravine to which the species gives its name, and having circled unwillingly round, with a ghastly scream and a flagging wing, it had sunk down upon the pinnacle of a crag, not four yards from the tree in which Arthur held his precarious station. Although still in some degree stupefied by torpor, it seemed encouraged by the motionless state of the young man to suppose him dead, or dying, and sat there and gazed at him, without displaying any of that apprehension which the fiercest animals usually entertain from the vicinity of man.

Having devoutly recommended himself to our Lady of Einsiedlen, of whom the legends of the Catholic Church form a

picture so amiable, Arthur, though every nerve still shook with
his agitation, and his heart throbbed with a violence that threatened to suffocate him, turned his thoughts and observations to
the means of effecting his escape. But, as he looked around
him, he became more and more sensible how much he was ener-
vated by the bodily injuries and the mental agony which he had
sustained during his late peril. He could not, by any effort of
which he was capable, fix his giddy and bewildered eyes on the
scene around him ; they seemed to reel till the landscape danced
along with them, and a motley chaos of thickets and tall cliffs,
which interposed between him and the ruinous Castle of Geierstein, mixed and whirled round in such confusion, that nothing
save the consciousness that such an idea was the suggestion of
partial insanity, prevented him from throwing himself from the
tree, as if to join the wild dance to which his disturbed brain
had given motion.

"Heaven be my protection!" said the unfortunate young
man, closing his eyes, in hopes, by abstracting himself from the
terrors of his situation, to compose his too active imagination,
"my senses are abandoning me!"

He became still more convinced that this was the case, when
a female voice, in a high-pitched but eminently musical accent,
was heard at no great distance, as if calling to him. He opened
his eyes once more, raised his head, and looked towards the
place from whence the sounds seemed to come, though far from
being certain that they existed, saving in his own disordered
imagination. The vision which appeared had almost confirmed
him in the opinion that his mind was unsettled, and his senses
in no state to serve him accurately.

Upon the very summit of a pyramidical rock that rose out
of the depth of the valley, was seen a female figure, so obscured

by mist, that only the outline could be traced. The form, reflected against the sky, appeared rather the undefined linea-
ments of a spirit than of a mortal maiden, for her person seemed
as light, and scarcely more opaque, than the thin cloud that
surrounded her pedestal. Arthur's first belief was, that the
Virgin had heard his vows, and had descended in person to his
rescue; and he was about to recite his Ave Maria, when the
voice again called to him, with the singular shrill modulation of
the mountain halloo, by which the natives of the Alps can hold
conference with each other from one mountain ridge to another,
across ravines of great depth and width.

While he debated how to address this unexpected apparition, it disappeared from the point which it at first occupied,
and presently after became again visible, perched on the cliff
out of which projected the tree in which Arthur had taken
refuge. Her personal appearance, as well as her dress, made it
then apparent that she was a maiden of these mountains, familiar with their dangerous paths. He saw that a beautiful young
woman stood before him, who regarded him with a mixture of
pity and wonder.

"Stranger," she at length said, "who are you, and whence
come you?"

"I am a stranger, maiden, as you justly term me," answered
the young man, raising himself as well as he could. "I left
Lucerne this morning, with my father and a guide. I parted
with them not three furlongs from hence. May it please you,
gentle maiden, to warn them of my safety, for I know my father
will be in despair upon my account?"

"Willingly," said the maiden; "but I think my uncle, or
some one of my kinsmen, must have already found them, and
will prove faithful guides. Can I not aid you?—are you

wounded—are you hurt? We were alarmed by the fall of a rock—ay, and yonder it lies, a mass of no ordinary size."

As the Swiss maiden spoke thus, she approached so close to the verge of the precipice, and looked with such indifference into the gulf, that the sympathy which connects the actor and spectator upon such occasions brought back the sickness and vertigo from which Arthur had just recovered, and he sunk back into his former more recumbent posture, with something like a faint groan.

The maiden looked on him anxiously, and with much interest, as, raising himself cautiously, and moving along the trunk of the tree, which lay nearly horizontal from the rock, and seemed to bend as he changed his posture, the youth at length stood upright, within what, on level ground, had been but an extended stride to the cliff on which the Swiss maiden stood. But instead of being a step to be taken on the level and firm earth, it was one which must cross a dark abyss, at the bottom of which a torrent surged and boiled with incredible fury. Arthur's knees knocked against each other, his feet became of lead, and seemed no longer at his command; and he experienced, in a stronger degree than ever, that unnerving influence, which those who have been overwhelmed by it in a situation of like peril never can forget, and which others, happily strangers to its power, may have difficulty even in comprehending.

The young woman discerned his emotion, and foresaw its probable consequences. As the only mode in her power to restore his confidence, she sprung lightly from the rock to the stem of the tree, on which she alighted with the ease and security of a bird, and in the same instant back to the cliff; and extending her arm to the stranger, " My arm," she said, " is but a slight balustrade; yet do but step forward with resolution, and you will find it as secure as the battlement of Berne." But shame now overcame terror so much, that Arthur, declining assistance which he could not have accepted without feeling lowered in his own eyes, took heart of grace, and successfully achieved the formidable step which placed him upon the same cliff with his kind assistant.

To seize her hand and raise it to his lips, in affectionate token of gratitude and respect, was naturally the youth's first action; nor was it possible for the maiden to have prevented him from doing so, without assuming a degree of prudery foreign to her character, and occasioning a ceremonious debate upon a matter of no great consequence, where the scene of action was a rock scarce five feet long by three in width, and which looked down upon a torrent roaring some hundred feet below.

LADY AUGUSTA BERKELY.

ARRIVED, as it appeared to the lady, on more level ground, they proceeded on their singular road by a course which appeared neither direct nor easy, and through an atmosphere which was close to a smothering degree, and felt at the same time damp and disagreeable, as if from the vapors of a new-made grave. Her guide again spoke:

"Bear up, Lady Augusta, for a little longer, and continue to endure that atmosphere which must be one day common to us all. By the necessity of my situation, I must resign my present office to your original guide, and can only give you my assurance, that neither he nor any one else, shall offer you the least incivility or insult—and on this you may rely, on the faith of a man of-honor."

He placed her, as he said these words, upon the soft turf, and, to her infinite refreshment, made her sensible that she was once more in the open air, and free from the smothering atmosphere which had before oppressed her like that of a charnel-house. At the same time, she breathed in a whisper an anxious wish that she might be permitted to disencumber herself from the folds of the mantle, which excluded almost the power of breathing, though intended only to prevent her seeing by what road she travelled. She immediately found it unfolded, agreeably to her request, and hastened, with uncovered eyes, to take note of the scene around her.

It was overshadowed by thick oak trees, among which stood some remnants of buildings, or what might have seemed such, being perhaps the same in which she had been lately wandering. A clear fountain of living water bubbled forth from under the twisted roots of one of those trees, and offered the lady the opportunity of a draught of the pure element, and in which she also bathed her face, which had received more than one scratch in the course of her journey, in spite of the care, and almost the tenderness, with which she had latterly been borne along. The cool water speedily stopped the bleeding of those trifling injuries, and the application served at the same time to recall the scattered senses of the damsel herself. Her first idea was, whether an attempt to escape, if such should appear possible, was not advisable. A moment's reflection, however, satisfied her that such a scheme was not to be thought of; and such second thoughts were confirmed by the approach of the gigantic form of the huntsman Turnbull, the rough tones of whose voice were heard before his figure was obvious to her eye.

"Were you impatient for my return, fair lady? Such as I," he continued, in an ironical tone of voice, "who are foremost in the chase of wild stags and sylvan cattle, are not in use to lag behind, when fair ladies, like you, are the objects of pursuit; and if I am not so constant in my attendance as you might expect, believe me, it is because I was engaged in another matter, to which I must sacrifice for a little even the duty of attending on you."

"I offer no resistance," said the lady; "forbear, however, in discharging thy duty, to augment my uneasiness by thy conversation, for thy master hath pledged me his word that he will not suffer me to be alarmed or ill treated."

" Nay, fair one," replied the huntsman, " I ever thought it was fit to make interest by soft words with fair ladies ; but if you like it not, I have no such pleasure in hunting for fine holyday terms, but that I can with equal ease hold myself silent. Come, then, since we must wait upon this lover of yours ere morning closes, and learn his last resolution touching a matter which is become so strangely complicated, I will hold no more intercourse with you as a female, but talk to you as a person of sense, although an Englishwoman."

" You will," replied the lady, " best fulfil the intentions of those by whose orders you act, by holding no society with me whatever, otherwise than is necessary in the character of guide."

The man lowered his brows, yet seemed to assent to what the Lady of Berkely proposed, and remained silent as they for some time pursued their course, each pondering over their own share of meditation, which probably turned upon matters essentially different. At length the loud blast of a bugle was heard at no great distance from the unsocial fellow-travellers. " That is the person we seek," said Turnbull ; " I know his blast from any other who frequents this forest, and my orders are to bring you to speech of him."

The blood darted rapidly through the lady's veins at the thought of being thus unceremoniously presented to the knight, in whose favor she had confessed a rash preference more agreeable to the manners of those times, when exaggerated sentiments often inspired actions of extravagant generosity, than in our days, when every thing is accounted absurd which does not turn upon a motive connected with the immediate selfish interests of

29

the actor himself. When Turnbull, therefore, winded his horn, as if in answer to the blast which they had heard, the lady was disposed to fly at the first impulse of shame and of fear. Turnbull perceived her intention, and caught hold of her with no very gentle grasp, saying, "Nay, lady, it is to be understood that you play your own part in the drama, which, unless you continue on the stage, will conclude unsatisfactorily to us all, in a combat at outrance between your lover and me, when it will appear which of us is most worthy of your favor."

"I will be patient," said the lady, bethinking her that even this strange man's presence, and the compulsion which he appeared to use towards her, was a sort of excuse to her female scruples for coming into the presence of her lover—at least of her first appearance before him in a disguise which her feelings confessed was not extremely decorous, or reconcilable to the dignity of her sex.

ZILIA DE MONCADA.

WHEN they entered the room, the unhappy young woman was on her knees, beside an easy chair, her face in a silk wrapper that was hung over it. The man called Monçada uttered a single word; by the accent it might have been something equiv-alent to *wretch;* but none knew its import. The female gave a convulsive shudder, such as that by which a half-dying soldier is affected on receiving a second wound. But without minding her emotion, Monçada seizing her by the arm, and with little gentleness raised her to her feet, on which she seemed to stand only because she was supported by his strong grasp. He then pulled from her face the mask which she had hitherto worn. The poor creature still endeavored to shroud her face, by cover-ing it with her left hand, as the manner in which she was held prevented her from using the aid of the right. With little effort her father secured that hand also, which, indeed, was of itself far too little to serve the purpose of concealment, and showed her beautiful face burning with blushes and covered with tears.

"You, Alcalde, and you, Surgeon," he said to Lawford and Gray, with a foreign action and accent, "this woman is my daughter, the same Zilia Monçada who is signal'd in that protocol. Make way, and let me carry her where her crimes may be atoned for."

"Are you that person's daughter?" said Lawford to the lady.

"She understands no English," said Gray; and addressing his patient in French, conjured her to let him know whether she was that man's daughter or not, assuring her of protection if the fact were otherwise. The answer was murmured faintly, but was too distinctly intelligible—"He was her father."

All farther title of interference seemed now ended. The messenger arrested his prisoner, and, with some delicacy, required the assistance of the females to get her conveyed to the carriage in waiting.

Gray again interfered.—"You will not," he said, "separate the mother and the infant?"

Zilia de Monçada heard the question, (which, being addressed to the father, Gray had inconsiderately uttered in French,) and it seemed as if it recalled to her recollection the existence of the helpless creature to which she had given birth, forgotten for a moment amongst the accumulated horrors of her father's presence. She uttered a shriek, expressing poignant grief, and turned her eyes on her father with the most intense supplication.

"To the parish with the bastard!"—said Monçada; while the helpless mother sunk lifeless into the arms of the females, who had now gathered round her.

"That will not pass, sir," said Gideon.—"If you are father to that lady, you must be grandfather to the helpless child; and you must settle in some manner for its future provision, or refer us to some responsible person."

Monçada looked towards Lawford, who expressed himself satisfied of the propriety of what Gray said.

" I object not to pay for whatever the wretched child may require," said he ; " and if you, sir," addressing Gray, " choose to take charge of him, and breed him up, you shall have what will better your living."

The Doctor was about to refuse a charge so uncivilly offered ; but after a moment's reflection, he replied, " I think so indifferently of the proceedings I have witnessed, and of those concerned in them, that if the mother desires that I should retain the charge of this child, I will not refuse to do so."

Monçada spoke to his daughter, who was just beginning to recover from her swoon, in the same language in which he had first addressed her. The proposition which he made seemed highly acceptable, as she started from the arms of the females, and, advancing to Gray, seized his hand, kissed it, bathed it in her tears, and seemed reconciled, even in parting with her child, by the consideration, that the infant was to remain under his guardianship.

" Good, kind man," she said in her indifferent French, " you have saved both mother and child."

The father, meanwhile, with mercantile deliberation, placed in Mr. Lawford's hands notes and bills to the amount of a thousand pounds, which he stated was to be vested for the child's use, and advanced in such portions as his board and education might require. In the event of any correspondence on his account being necessary, as in case of death or the like, he directed that communication should be made to Signor Matthias Moncada, under cover to a certain banking-house in London.

"But beware," he said to Gray, "how you trouble me about these concerns, unless in case of absolute necessity."

"You need not fear, sir," replied Gray; "I have seen nothing to-day which can induce me to desire a more intimate correspondence with you than may be indispensable."

The father then spoke to his daughter a few stern words, which she heard with an air of mingled agony and submission.

"I have given her a few minutes to see and weep over the miserable being which has been the seal of her dishonor," said the stern father. "Let us retire and leave her alone.—You," to the messenger," watch the door of the room on the outside."

Gray, Lawford, and Moncada, retired to the parlor accordingly, where they waited in silence, each busied with his own reflections, till, within the space of half an hour, they received information that the lady was ready to depart.

"It is well," replied Moncada; "I am glad she has yet sense enough left to submit to that which needs must be."

So saying, he ascended the stair, and returned, leading down his daughter, now again masked and veiled. As she passed Gray, she uttered the words—"My child, my child!" in a tone of unutterable anguish; then entered the carriage, which was drawn up as close to the door of the Doctor's house as the little enclosure would permit, and the carriage drove rapidly off taking the road which leads to Edinburgh.

THE END.

www.ingramcontent.com/pod-product-compliance
Lightning Source LLC
Chambersburg PA
CBHW020504270326
41926CB00008B/736